W9-BIH-125

I Killed June Cleaver

Modern Moms Shatter the Myth of Perfect Parenting

Edited by Deborah Werksman

Hysteria Publications
A Division of Sourcebooks, Inc.
Naperville, IL • Bridgeport, CT

Quotations in this book come from the following sources:
Women's Lip: Outrageous, Irreverent and Just Plain Hilarious Quotes edited
by Roz Warren, Sourcebooks, 1998;
The Beacon Book of Quotations by Women, compiled by Rosalie Maggio,
Beacon Press, 1992;
GlibQuips: Funny Words by Funny Women, edited by Roz Warren, The
Crossing Press, 1994;
The Sun, April 1995.

Published by Sourcebooks, Inc.

Naperville Office
P.O. Box 372
Naperville, IL 60566
630-961-3900
Fax: 630-961-2168

Bridgeport Office
P.O. Box 38581
Bridgeport, CT 06605
203-333-9399
Fax: 203-367-7188

ISBN 1-887166-47-5

Printed and bound in the United States of America
10 9 8 7 6 5 4 3 2 1

This book is dedicated to my children,
Kayla and Jacob. I wouldn't be a parent without them.

ACKNOWLEDGMENTS

To my wonderful, happy family, especially my husband and soulmate, Jeff Yoder, who makes everything possible. Thanks to my mom for loving me so much, especially during those two insufferable phases, adolescence and early motherhood, and to my dad, with whom I can talk about anything. To my brother and sister-in-law Mark and Leslie, and their brood; my sister and brother-in-law Rochelle and Doug; my aunts, uncles, and my precious cousins, among whom I count my best friends.

To all my friends, who support me with love and affection.

To all my colleagues at Sourcebooks, who are both brilliant and truly fun to work with.

And finally, to all the talented, funny women writers and cartoonists out there, whose gift to the world is giggles. It is a privilege to edit and publish your work.

Contents

Collective Wisdom

Mommyrella *by Cathi Turow*   3

The Collective Wisdom of Mothers on Drugs
    by Linda Kantner   7

I Killed June Cleaver: Toward a New Model
    of Mothering *by Colleen Kilcoyne*   14

Animals with an Attitude *by Catherine Conant*   18

Mom and Dad Are Doin' It! (Or Trying To)
    by Betsy Banks Epstein   23

Sizzling *by Donna Black*   27

What They Don't Teach You in Childbirth Class

Curse of the Mommy *by Cathy Crimmins*   34

    Part I: Nesting with Sheetrock

    Part II: Biological Options

What They Don't Teach You in Childbirth Class
  by April Burk   42

The Nursing Section

Lactation's Lament *by Joan Scoggin*   48

The Nursing Section for Me, Please *by Roz Warren*   50

Lactation Obfuscation *by Carol Delaney*   53

Ask Dr. Baby

Night-Owl *by Janet Ruth Heller*   58

Ask Dr. Baby *by Alison J. Conte*   59

Truth and the Consequences *by Donna Black*   64

The Family Dinner Hour

The McSecret *by Lauren Andreano*   70

In Celebration of the Family
  Dinner Hour *by Joan Scoggin*   74

A Child's Garden of Delights *by Sally Curd*   77

Contents

Spit-Shining the Kids

Laundry Mom *by Joan Scoggin* 86

Keeping 'Em Clean *by Lynne Ewing Mayesh* 89

Spit-Shining the Kids *by Barbara A. Tyler* 93

Cleanliness *by Angela D. Conroy* 97

The Once-a-Month Housewife *by Anne Hodge* 100

It's Wednesday and I Don't Have
    Any Clean Underwear *by Sherri Jones Rivers* 104

Observations

Children's Car Pool Accord *by Madeleine Begun Kane* 110

Through the Bathroom Door *by Angela D. Conroy* 116

The Broken Foot *by Debra Godfrey* 119

Observations on a Rare Bird *by Alice Kolega* 124

Why It Takes Mom a Week to Get Over
    the 24-Hour Flu *by Angela D. Conroy* 134

The Alien at My House

The Alien at My House *by Renee Carr*   140

Teenonics *by Angela D. Conroy*   144

How to Recognize the Father of Teenagers
    by Ina Valeria Doyle   147

Queen of the Road *by Judith Marks-White*   148

The YA Return

It's All Greek to Me *by Pat Miller*   154

It's Hard to Say Goodbye *by Effin Older*   159

The Dreadlock Suite: Tales to Relieve a
    Mother's Distress *by Shirlee Sky Hoffman*   163

The Scent of Cash *by Mary A. Harding*   172

The YA Return *by Ina Valeria Doyle*   174

Collective Wisdom

What we owe our parents is
the bill presented to us by
our children.

—*Nancy Friday*

Mommyrella

Cathi Turow

Once upon a time, there was a mom who was overwhelmed. She lived with her husband, son, and two step-daughters. She was an architect with her own firm, "Creative Castle Concepts." Since she was responsible for running the business, raising the kids, managing the house, cooking the meals, doing the laundry, and polishing the silverware, everyone called her "Mommyrella."

As the fairy tale goes, on the day before the first day of school, Mommyrella came home early from work. Before she could put down her briefcase, her son shouted, "Mommyrella! I need the notebook with the aliens on it today!" Her younger daughter screamed, "Mommyrella! You still didn't buy me the pencils that glow in the dark!" Her teenage daughter wailed, "Mommyrella! You said you'd give me money for a new bookbag!!"

"Don't worry, children," Mommyrella said kindly, "I haven't forgotten."

Just as Mommyrella was about to schlep the kids out for all that they needed, she got a fax. It said, "Hear ye, Hear ye: The prince is planning to renovate his castle. All architects in the land are invited to present their plans, but you must arrive at the palace by 6:00 P.M. tonight."

"Oh," sighed the starry-eyed Mommyrella, "how I wish I could meet with the prince." "But Mommyrella!" her son interrupted, "You have to take me to soccer tonight!" Her daughter chimed in, "And I have gymnastics tonight! If I miss the first class, I won't make friends!" Her teenage daughter shouted the loudest, "You swore you'd drive me to the movies! And then you're taking me to the mall for new shoes. Remember?" Mommyrella nodded. "I remember," she said.

And so Mommyrella bought the kids all their school supplies, dropped them off where they needed to be, and zoomed home to throw in a load of laundry. Then, by some miracle, she realized she actually had forty-three minutes to herself. She could zip over to the palace before anybody had to be picked up! But when she looked down wearily at her sweats and sneakers, she moaned, "I'll never have time to shower and change and make it to the palace."

Suddenly, Mommyrella's Fairy Godmother appeared! She waved her wand and turned Mommyrella's sweats to a stunning suit and her high tops to high heels. "Now you can go to the palace in style," the Fairy Godmother said with a smile. "But remember! When the clock strikes seven, you have to pick up your son at soccer!"

Mommyrella was the last to arrive at the palace. Though the prince had not been thrilled with any of the plans he'd seen, when he laid eyes on Mommyrella's plan, he fell in love. Just as they were deciding which faucets would look best on the royal Jacuzzi, the clock struck seven. Mommyrella popped up and dashed out of the palace! The prince called after her, "Wait! I didn't get your business card!" Poor Mommyrella was in too much of a hurry to hear him. As she rushed down the palace steps, her shoe fell off. She didn't even notice.

Mommyrella picked up all three kids on time. They dashed to buy her teenage daughter new shoes as fast as they could. But alas, the mall had closed.

Early the next morning, Mommyrella was hustling and bustling around the house, trying to get her kids ready for the first day of school. Her teenage daughter was still brooding about the new shoes. "You always break your promises," she screamed at Mommyrella. "I hate you."

Just then, there was a knock at the door. It was the prince— holding Mommyrella's shoe. He declared, "Whoever fits this shoe shall renovate my palace." The teenage daughter took one look at the high heel, gasped, and cried, "Wow! Great shoe!"

The prince was about to try the shoe on Mommyrella, when she said, "Try it on my daughter. We wear the same size."

The shoe fit her daughter perfectly. Mommyrella took the matching shoe from her bathrobe pocket and placed it on her daughter's other foot. "Thanks Mom," cried her daughter, "I love you sooooo much."

And so, as the fairy tale ends, the bus pulled up, all three kids got on happily, and Mommyrella got the renovation job at the palace. The moral of the story? Somehow, everything gets done.

Cathi Turow has been a staff writer for Sesame Street for the past fifteen years, and has won ten Emmy awards. She also writes a regular humor column for the parenting newsletter "F.A.C.E. I.T. Today" which can be seen on the Web at www.faceitinc.com. The story "Mommyrella" originally appeared on the Working Mom's Internet Refuge, www.moms-refuge.com.

The Collective Wisdom
of Mothers on Drugs

Linda Kantner

Baby-Mom Togetherness Class met at my house this week. We are an upwardly mobile group—socially, politically, and ecologically correct, thus our need for support. Before our children were born, we ran humanitarian organizations, volunteered in Cambodia, studied Japanese, and went white-water rafting. Now, we are mothers.

We meet weekly at Christ Evangelical Church although none of us claims a religious alliance. We get the cozy daycare cheap and they let us eat the day-old donuts. The saints have looked worn and tired since Easter and attendance is down, so the parish decided to paint. One clear-thinking mom expressed concern about the fumes befuddling the developing brains of our infants. We voted unanimously to meet at my house.

We never miss a week. As new mothers we are in a steady state of bewilderment and need the group for grounding and reality testing. We all have experienced the humiliation of not remembering our area code or the name of the current vice president. On one particularly bad day, none of us could remember the author of *The Female Eunuch*. We quiz each other to keep our minds sharp and to commiserate over mental lapses. We reassure each other that our confusion is hormonal and not permanent. Kegel exercises are done as a team to Mr. Rogers' theme song, "Would You Be My Neighbor?" Kegels help prevent the squirt of urine that now comes with unexpected outbursts of laughter or sneezing.

The seriousness of our task weighs heavily. There is the question of property rights to our breasts. Are they put away for the night after the ten o'clock news or brought out for 2:00 A.M. feedings? We are alert for any signs of moral development, athletic ability, and first words. The group is competitive but compassionate: "Almost everyone walks eventually. You shouldn't worry."

This week, away from the watchful eyes of the saints, our conversation took a dramatic turn. For a moment we almost became what we once had been.

"I have always wanted to try smoking opium."

"I bet you've never even tried smoking pot."

"No. But I've never really wanted to smoke pot. Pot is so pedestrian. Opium is mystical. It gets you in touch with your karma."

"So does labor."

"Labor got me in touch with my hemorrhoids."

"I'd try opium, but where are the opium dens? You have to smoke opium in a den, otherwise it just isn't the same."

"We could do it in our den."

"You have a family room, not a den. There is a Ping Pong table in it and pictures of hunting dogs carrying dead ducks. An opium den would have oriental tapestries on the wall."

"There is a wall hanging."

"It's a macramé bird nest."

"I'd worry about the kids getting secondhand smoke."

"One little toke of secondhand smoke turned Johnnie's brain into a joke. Oops. I'm a little loose—too much coffee, not enough sleep. Do you have any decaf?"

"Atmosphere makes all the difference with opium. That's the good thing about beer, it goes with everything and increases milk supply."

"I think Nicholas may be about to eat a dandelion. My husband put chemicals on the yard while I was napping, I don't know what got into him. One dandelion probably wouldn't hurt but I just wanted you to know."

"Nick, honey, no dandelions. That's a Mr. Yuk. Here's a puffed wheat bar, that will be 'nummy.' He puts everything in his mouth, what can I do? I'm starting to think he'll be a chef when he grows up."

"Or a goat."

"We would need sitar music if we smoked opium."

"I can help there. We have some Sesame Street tapes with Big Bird on guitar. He also plays the kazoo."

"No, not guitar. Sitar music. Eastern music. Ravi Shankar, Hari Krishna, all that."

"What about tabouli?"

"What about it?"

"It's eastern. We could eat tabouli while we smoke opium. Maybe drink a nice Chardonnay?"

"Where are we going to get opium? The only drug I take any more is calcium for my milk. Which reminds me, does Tommy ever bite you? Nicky bit me on the neck the other day and it looks like I have a hickey."

"I haven't had a hickey in years. I'd be glad to have one no matter where it came from. Could I hold him a minute?"

"I know someone who takes drugs. They're prescription so they probably aren't any fun. You can't smoke Valium, can you?"

"I can't smoke any drugs right now. I'm in training for a mother-daughter marathon."

"Julia's two months old, how can she be in a marathon?"

"I'm carrying her on my back in a pack. I'll sling her to the front when she needs to nurse."

"You must be on drugs already."

"Running is a natural high. You should try it. We could organize a group and run in a pack, like wolves."

"I'd be as likely to fly north and live in a swamp like a loon."

"Opium grows wild, it's probably good for you. Smoking it once wouldn't destroy your lungs."

"It might stunt our growth and give us wrinkles."

"Good, I don't want to grow anymore. I'd have to get all new clothes and remarry a taller man. It would be easier to smoke."

"The man doesn't need to be taller than the woman."

"That's right. He just needs to be tall enough to load the washing machine himself."

"We'll need to get a hookah."

"In the '60s I wore a necklace made of pookah. My boyfriend Dwight gave it to me."

"I'm talking about a water pipe, a hookah, like in the movie *Alice in Wonderland*."

"We don't rent videos, they all perpetuate sex role stereotypes. *Cinderella*, *Sleeping Beauty*, and *Snow White* are all waiting for a prince to save them. It's disgusting. Next you'll be buying Totally Hair Barbie, My First Bra, and Glitter Nails. Where will it end?"

"Where do you get those nails? Mine are a mess."

"You're right about the videos, it never occurred to me, I'm so ashamed. Do you think Libby needs therapy?"

"I doubt if the information is stored in long-term memory; she's only ten months old, right? You caught it in time."

"And the opium smoke will probably kill off any remaining brain cells she has."

"Tommy has a water pipe but it's plastic, for blowing bubbles. I'm afraid it would melt if we tried to smoke anything in it, and he's awfully attached to it. That ravenous oral stage, you know."

"We'll get one at a head shop."

"Do they still have those? I thought they went out of business when everyone owned a mood ring."

"My ring always told me I was depressed so I got rid of it and felt much better. Why don't we just eat the opium. With breast-feeding I'm always hungry. We could bake it into brownies."

"Or a nice opium cheese spread on a Trisket. I'm watching my weight."

"I'll bring beer. I've heard your mouth gets incredibly dry afterwards."

"That's pot. We're going to feel really tired and crave sex."

"I don't want to crave sex when I'm really tired. What fun will that be?"

"Imagine this, we're sitting in the basement in La-Z-Boy recliners, listening to Big Bird on the guitar, drinking Budweiser and hallucinating on the pine paneling. Then, due to extreme exhaustion, we'll fall asleep with babies on our chests, cheese spread on our lips, and fantasies about sex with Bert and Ernie since they are the only men we see anymore."

Reality intrudes, our fantasy drifts and fades. A puff of smoke. How could it be? How would it be?

Opium Smoking Moms.

Linda Kantner's most recent work has appeared in Sacred Ground: Stories about Home (Milkweed Press). *Her work also has appeared in anthologies and regional collections.*

I Killed June Cleaver:
Toward a New Model of Mothering

Colleen Kilcoyne

I've killed June Cleaver. I've killed June Cleaver and finally I know some mothering peace.

I'm tentatively claiming some mothering pride. The truth of my mothering history shocks me: I have not been a bad mother; I have been a bad June!

How could this have happened? How did June become my model? For all of my reading and lecturing on parenting skills, I was poisoned unaware, oblivious to her insidious penetration into my life.

There have been so many ways I've been a bad June...

- I have always thought that the playground is boring.
- I hate to bake.
- Barely verbal, my kids knew how to hand sign, "You drive me crazy," and "You're buggin' my butt."
- I cry out loud when they really hurt my feelings.
- I taught them rock and roll; they know every word to "Wooly Bully."

There are many more June sins to list, but that short confession has done me good.

The reality of motherhood was really tough for me. Soon after my son Josh was born I called my closest friend Ronnie, crying. He asked, "What's wrong?" and I sobbed out, "I miss my old life." And I did, intensely. And that, I think, explains part of my struggle in trying to be June. I have expected myself to act as a mother in ways that I never would as a person.

I have never been a patient person, but I thought I should be a patient Mom. Now I'll admit that in being a Mom there's nothing wrong with pushing your patience limit a bit for your children's sake, but there were situations and activities that I should never have attempted because, quite simply, they reeked of June.

Two summers ago, Josh proposed a "School's Out" celebration with ten of his schoolmates. I really don't enjoy large groups of children so I should have known it was a June activity at which I was destined to fail. The kids were grumpy because it was ninety-eight degrees and all of the games were planned for outdoors. The boys and girls decided to fight and expected me to be the referee. Josh came undone when the nine other children wouldn't do what he wanted because, "It's my party!" The party ended for me with a very early (not five o'clock yet!) glass of Chardonnay and a splitting headache.

Killing June has been very freeing. Last summer, my husband Don, son Josh, and my daughter Sara, wanted to go camping, and they wanted me along. I loathe camping; for me it's right up there with blood tests and ironing for its entertainment value. Still, I was attracted by the promise of quality family time and wanted to figure out a way to make it work.

We drove down to Yogi Bear's Campground in Sturbridge, Massachusetts. After selecting a site, we unloaded the car and began the long hard task of setting up the tent. Having managed that, we rewarded ourselves with a swim in the pond and a warming bask on the beach. Peanut butter and jelly sandwiches tasted great as we sat and talked at the big old picnic table next to our site. After lunch, we went on a nature hike all through the campground. We arrived back with our arms full of various rocks, leaves, and, being good earthkeepers, a sack of trash other people had left behind. With great relish we gathered wood, built a fine campfire, and roasted hot dogs. The requisite marshmallows topped off our meal. As darkness fell, I hugged and kissed each member of my family; I told them I loved them, but not camping.

I then drove a mile down the road and checked into the Sturbridge Coach Motor Lodge. The roar of passing trucks, not the chirping of a million crickets, was the lullaby I preferred; I fell asleep with a smile.

I killed June Cleaver. Should'a done it long ago.

Colleen Kilcoyne is a freelance writer based in Lexington, Massachusetts. She makes her home there with her husband and children, ages 12 and 13. Her work has appeared in The Boston Globe, The Boston Parents' Paper, Mothering Magazine, *and other publications.*

Animals with an Attitude

Catherine Conant

At the moment in your life when you move from the group defined as "non-parents" into the group defined as "parents," the world beats a path to your door with volumes of worthwhile/worthless advice. Suddenly, at the first public announcement that your family is expanding, everybody is an expert and the temptation to offer another bit of homespun wisdom is too good to resist.

"Remember, the baby will let you know what she needs," as if there was a baby born who doesn't love to play "Guess Why I'm Screaming." Or, "We have always trusted our kids to make the right decisions." This comes from the parents of the kid who just showed you a face full of piercings and a tattoo.

But no matter how much advice, useful and otherwise, well-wishers give, when it comes to the subject of kids and pets, the silence is deafening. Well, I'll be the one to tell you that what starts out looking like an ordinary baby will very quickly grow up to be Noah of the Ark, who will feel directed by God to collect at least two of everything that walks, flies, crawls, slithers, or sheds.

I don't take pride in the fact, but since you ask, no, I don't like pets. It's not my fault. I was raised by a woman who believed that if you invite animals into the house, vermin come along for the ride. Where there are vermin, moral decay isn't far behind, and the next thing you know you're drinking milk straight from the carton and headed for hell in a hand basket.

Not that my deep-seated distaste for sharing my house with other species made the slightest impression on my children. As soon as they were able to lisp the sentences, "Can we bring him home Mommy, can we? We'll take good care of him, promise." I began paying hard cash for an assortment of amphibians, birds, and countless tiny rodents who grabbed the first opportunity to disappear into the heating ducts. Not one of these critters had the decency to make its own living arrangements. I had to purchase home, food, appropriate exercise equipment, toys, and grooming aids. This compulsion to buy creatures and bring them home to live in cages that take up valuable counter space will last until the day you come to discover that the only animal your daughter is interested in is named "Chad" and reeks of testosterone.

Don't try and sell me on the "pets teach responsibility" hogwash. We both know, if it eats, it poops. If you'd like the challenge of the weekly ritual of nagging a child to empty a loaded litter box, be my guest. I'm saving my energy for talking my child out of skydiving.

Since it is practically impossible to raise a child in this country without also investing in animals and their accessories, please feel free to keep this handy animal guide so that when you're on your way down to make a purchase at Ye Olde Pet Shoppe, at least you will know what the choices are.

Animals with Blank Expressions

Lizards, salamanders, chameleons, iguanas, and all snakes. Their entire range of expression is limited to blinking. They need to be kept warm, so you have a perpetual night light with an expensive bulb. They can stay in the same position for long periods of time, and owners have been known to feed pets who had been dead for several days. A subspecies is fish. Think of them only as moving interior decoration.

Animals Who Reproduce Compulsively

Hamsters, gerbils, mice, rabbits, rats, guinea pigs. Having limited imagination, these animals can only think of two things. The other thing is getting out of their cage so that they can die in the walls of your house. While you may think you can share the "miracle of life" with your kids, no parenting book in the world offers guidance on how to explain to a hysterical child why Mr. and Mrs. Wiggles just ate their babies.

Animals Who Believe You Are Living in Their House

Cats, dogs, some birds. Due to the fact that greeting card companies now offer cards to mark important events in your dog's or cat's life, these animals feel that you are lucky to be living with them, and don't you forget it, pal. Their tendency is to rummage through the garbage, deposit huge amounts of dander on furniture, and support large flea colonies (see vermin). Birds, while less likely to sharpen their claws on the couch, will indulge in aerial attacks and foul language.

Animals with an Attitude

Weasels, chinchillas, hedgehogs, minks, geckoes. Fifty years ago, these critters would never have been household pets, and they know it. Just looking at them you get the sense that if they could just get to a telephone they would be out of there before you could say, "Greenpeace." Given to fits of pique, they are nocturnal in nature, and will get even with you for keeping them in captivity by staying up all night making a racket.

Keep in mind, whatever style of animal you do purchase, there is a pretty good chance it will suddenly depart this mortal coil at a supremely inconvenient moment, leaving you to make funeral arrangements and haul its former home to the basement.

If your child insists on having a pet, consider a horse. Horses live in their own house, never scratch on the door to come in, and will give you more than enough fertilizer to grow great tomatoes.

Catherine Conant is a Connecticut-based freelance writer and storyteller.

Mom and Dad Are Doin' It! (Or Trying To)

Betsy Banks Epstein

Every self-respecting women's magazine currently on the newsstands has an article on sex: innovative positions, imaginative places, aromatic oils, private signals, the significance of what you do for afterplay, and of course that old favorite—the importance of foreplay. What baffles me is that these magazines are aimed at an audience that has precious few spare moments to contemplate the intricacies of intercourse.

Take my friend Anna. She's living in a two-bedroom apartment with three kids under the age of seven. Two children share a room and the toddler is sleeping in a portacrib in the master bedroom, lurking behind the oriental screen that Anna snagged from her mother-in-law's gift shop. Anna and her husband satisfy themselves while hiding under their bed, since they're afraid the bouncing boxspring will awaken the baby, and they're terrified by the notion of their son popping up from behind the screen and watching them. One of Anna's child study manuals claims that this could compromise a child's sexual development for life. I suppose you could give Anna and her husband credit for a creative location.

When my kids were young, they didn't understand the social etiquette of knocking before they entered. To make matters worse, my husband and I had a bedroom door without a lock. Our private signal was that one of us would gesture in the direction of the marble slab which my husband had attempted to sculpt during an adult education class. This piece of stone had a seat of honor on our bureau. When it was placed on the floor in front of our bedroom door, no forty-pound child could push past it. I've often thought that my husband's most romantic anniversary gift was a down comforter, a furry mattress pad, a silk robe, and a brass lock for our bedroom door.

My neighbor Mindy spent a few days at a health spa last summer and came home with decadent body creams and atmospheric candles. She's got two teenage sons, so one would think that she could have lots of privacy during the evening. When these boys are not gorging themselves in front of the refrigerator or taking twenty-minute showers, they're behind their closed doors blaring heavy-metal music, talking on the phone, or languishing on their beds staring off into space. The catch is that they spring to life around 11:00 P.M., just as Mindy and her husband are settling down to cuddle in front of the news. They choose this moment to need their mother to prove a theorem or their father to critique an essay. Mindy encourages the communication with her sons, but she has trouble explaining the smelly candle beside her bed as her husband scrambles to pull on his boxers while he's slippery with lotion.

My sister-in-law Susan inquires, "Why don't people just lock their doors and say they're busy?" I've told her that it's hard to concentrate when you have a ten-year-old insistently knocking on the other side of that door. Worse still is when she hollers: "What are you two *doing* in there?" She's the real reason that I find the poll on people's favorite moves during afterplay so amusing. My husband and I race to cover ourselves up before letting her in.

Stan, my husband's business associate, claims that even when one's kids are away at college, you never know at what hour of the night they might call. He loves it when his wife is perched comfortably on top of him, and his daughter chooses that instant to phone home. "So...what's up with you guys?" she gaily begins when she's in the mood for a long chat.

I suppose the message is that there's ample opportunity for foreplay if you define it as the frustration of dashed opportunity or the endless dreaming of possibility. We could just explain to our kids that Mom and Dad are "doin' it." But even during these days of open discussions about AIDS, condoms, homosexuality, and heterosexuality—few children would believe it.

Betsy Banks Epstein is a mother of three and a freelance writer based in Cambridge, Massachusetts.

Sizzling

Donna Black

One of those "add spice to your sex life" magazine articles caught my attention recently with its guaranteed way to make me and my lovemate "sizzle" in sexual anticipation.

You see, with two young children running around in circles (which keeps their dad and me running around in circles), there's not a whole lot of time for anything else. And after all that running, any free moments we have are usually spent resting.

But sizzling sounded like such a red hot idea, I felt I had to give it a try. So I read the article's instructions and learned that, basically, all I had to do was get one tape recording of myself and my lovemate fooling around. And if I could tape it without my partner's knowledge, so much the better, for that was supposed to add even more sparks at playback time.

Not usually keen on having anything I do taped, I decided to put aside my misgivings, because, according to the article, once recorded, this cassette would be an instant aphrodisiac guaranteed to take us to new heights of afternoon (or morning, or nighttime) delight simply by playing it!

But before I could play it, I had to tape it, and before I could tape it, I had to dig up a tape recorder. Rummaging through my two-year-old's toy chest, I spotted my treasure: a bright yellow "Big Bird" recorder.

Next on the list was a blank tape. Unfortunately, this turned out to be a bit of a problem. The only cassette I could find held my four-year-old's tap recital song, but after a momentary twinge of guilt I erased it. Sure, we'd all miss hearing "On the Good Ship Lollipop," but to be honest, the choice between listening to Shirley Temple sing about her trip to the candy shop to eat all the sweets that I'm trying so hard to avoid and sizzling in sexual anticipation was not a hard one to make.

Having procured the necessary "pre-sizzle" components, all that was left was the taping. As luck would have it, an opportunity to perform the final deed presented itself on Saturday morning. For as soon as the kids ate their usual breakfast of cereal, toast, and bananas dipped in picante sauce (they're both native Texans), two sets of fat little legs wobbled out of the kitchen and into the living room to watch cartoons.

So, as the girls sat entranced with Bugs Bunny, Donald Duck, and all of their animated buddies, I quickly awakened my still-asleep spouse, and by mid-morning, both the tape recorder and newly-recorded cassette were safely hidden under my side of the bed (the only place I knew the kids wouldn't go because that's where monsters live). And although I had been able to keep it a secret from my spouse, I must admit I was really tempted to play it back immediately for myself. But then I remembered the article stressed the listening should be a "together" experience.

Knowing a long night of wining, dining, and being "together" wouldn't be possible with two toddlers close by, I called the grandparents. With just minimal begging and my notarized signature promising I'd replace whatever got broken, they agreed to babysit at their house.

The big night arrived and after finishing a lovely meal made even more special because we didn't have to dodge catapulting toddler-sized silverware or spend hours removing odd bits of food from the walls, table, and chairs, we retired to the bedroom.

I lit some candles (actually a whole bunch—we had only the small birthday kind) and put on my sexiest T-shirt. Well, OK, it was the same T-shirt I wore every night but at least I didn't accessorize with my thermal ankle socks and my face wasn't smeared with its normal glob of anti-aging wonder cream.

Winking seductively at my husband (he asked if I had something in my eye), I retrieved the tape recorder and cassette. While he jokingly asked if we were going to "tap off" our dinner (see, I told you we'd all miss the "Good Ship Lollipop"), I snuggled next to my lovemate, told him I had a grand surprise, and hit the "Play" button.

As it turns out, there was a heckuva surprise in store for both of us. I suppose we could have sizzled in sexual anticipation, but that's tough to do while doubled over in laughter with tears streaming from your eyes. You see, our aphrodisiac recording went something like this:

"Gee honey, guess it's been awhile, do you remember how to do this?"

"No, I really don't, but I read somewhere that you never forget how to ride a bike so maybe if we got on top of your old ten speed, this would come back as well."

"Mmmm, you smell really good—like strawberry jam—oh, wait a minute, you've got a big glob of it in your hair."

"Great. I was wondering where Annie left her piece of breakfast toast. Do you see any slightly burned bread nearby?"

"Oh no. Did you hear that?"

"Hear what? I found the bread, she stuck it in my ear."

"I thought I heard Brooke tell Annie she shouldn't have taken her diaper off because it was making the new couch wet."

"We'd better hurry and finish."

Knowing that laughter is the best medicine, I figure if we play the tape once a day, we'll never get sick. And when the offspring are finally grown and living elsewhere, we'll still be healthy enough to have our long, romantic interludes and, who knows, maybe we'll even sizzle.

Donna Black is a writer from Texas.

What They Don't Teach You in Childbirth Class

A woman came to ask the doctor
if a woman should have children
after 35. I said 35 children is
enough for any woman.

—*Gracie Allen*

Curse of the Mommy

Cathy Crimmins

Part I: Nesting with Sheetrock

One night, about the time the parasite had been an internal tenant for six months, I woke up in a cold sweat: "Where the hell are we going to put this kid?"

Lots of older people will tell you this is not an issue. "Oh, our oldest slept in a shoebox," they'll say. "We kept him under the kitchen sink until he was five—really, he was no problem at all. Babies don't take up much space, you know."

What a lot of poop. This is pre-MTV life they are talking about, not life as we now know it. When these people raised kids, their cars cost less than what an Aprica stroller sets you back nowadays. And when those prehistoric parents left the hospital, they took home a basic model infant, a kind of VW baby that didn't have a lot of stuff that went along with it. Already I could tell that my kid was going to be more like a loaded sedan. It would be coming home with four suitcases, massive amounts of infant stimulation equipment, and maybe even an exotic fish aquarium that it would get tired of after three months. This kid was going to need a room of its own, and I didn't have one.

Well, that wasn't exactly true. I had my home office, the only extra room in the house. I started noticing that the baby became particularly active whenever I was in there sitting at my desk. It was moving around in my belly, probably surveying its future digs. No doubt it was leafing through fetal catalogs for window treatments, or figuring out where to put the diaper pail. No way! I thought. The thing had squatter's rights in my womb, but it couldn't have my workplace. That was going too far. And so I did something that eventually threatened to destroy my health, my marriage, and my faith in the future of the human race. I called a contractor.

Now, with some distance of time, I can recognize that remodeling is an obsession of late pregnancy. But I had no idea back then where the nesting instinct would lead.

The demolition team came in the next day and started swinging. Before I knew it, I had a house with no walls that was resting precariously on a damaged soil pipe, and no hope of inhabiting the site until my kid was at least in kindergarten. And I hadn't even told my husband yet!

I stood crying amidst clouds of plaster dust that was surely on its way directly to that little set of fetal lungs inside me. "Geez,

Cath, you had a nice house, but it turned to shit," said the friendly plumber who had been called in to explain to me how lucky I was that the bathtub hadn't come crashing through the floor.

Was there some program, sort of like a Federal Witness Protection Program, for the hysterically pregnant? Could I just assume a new identity, start life anew in another town and hope that my husband would welcome the relief from Lamaze classes and eventually stop looking for me?

No, I was about to become a mother. I had to act maturely. I called my husband and began a logical explanation of why we would be living in the street in a refrigerator box for the next few months.

"Honey—remember how I told you that I never could learn to knit when I was in grade school? Well, I was thinking that if I had just learned to knit, I would have been able to knit little booties and hats and sweaters."

"Excuse me, who is this?" asked my husband on the other end.

"Well, the thing is, I think that my inability to knit little baby things and sort of get ready for our child's birth led me to kind of try to prepare for it in, well, sort of an inappropriate way."

"How much?" he asked, envisioning Parisian togs or West German perambulators. I broke down. "There's no walls anymore," I choked out. And then Louie, the carpenter, accidentally cut the phone wire as he was cutting into one of the joists.

Part II: Biological Options

I always expected to give birth in a hospital (preferably in a drug-induced stupor), but I didn't count on having personality conflicts with hospital staff. Actually, I wouldn't call them personality conflicts. More like personality nuclear wars.

I'm not a nice girl. I yell a lot when I get angry. Having to wait for hours on end in reception areas makes me angry. At my third prenatal appointment at the hospital, after about an hour cooling it on the delightful vinyl sofa, I began screaming and didn't stop until I got dragged into the inner office, where someone clapped a blood pressure cuff on me.

"You're going to be one of our high-risk patients," said the doctor, coming in and looking at the chart. "Your blood pressure is sky high."

"You're going to be at very low risk of ever seeing me again," I said, and left immediately (I never did return that hospital gown, either).

In the Yellow Pages under "Midwives" I found a listing for a "Little Birthing Center on the Prairie" type of place that was hyper-politically correct and never kept people waiting for more than five minutes, probably because they only had about twelve demented ex-hippie clients. A groovy quilt of a uterus and fallopian tubes hung on the wall, and the stirrups on the examination table were covered with gingham potholders. Everyone referred to my "partner" and didn't make any assumptions that the guy coming with me to childbirth classes had sired my kid. I liked this attitude because it meant I could always deny Al's paternity at any time during the labor process and feel comfortable.

This little brick farmhouse setup didn't have doctors or even a lot of bureaucratic red tape, but there was some paperwork involved in giving birth there. For weeks, the midwife hounded us to submit our "birth plan," a detailed document about exactly how we wanted our birthing experience to proceed.

There were so many elements I wanted to include as part of the optimal birth experience (like starting off with Mel Gibson at the conception). But it became a burden to decide between so many options. Delivering our baby at a birth center started to seem too much like buying a car or choosing bathroom fixtures.

The sperm donor and I spent hours debating the pros and cons of different birthing strategies. Should I sign up for Jacuzzi labor? After all, Flipper was born under water. So maybe our kid would have his own sitcom someday. But how could I enjoy sitting in a Jacuzzi for ten hours without a glass of white wine?

Then there was the option of giving birth standing up. This sounded good, because I wanted to look my thinnest as I was delivering. But a friend of mine had said that when her breathing exercises failed her, she spent most of labor hitting her husband really hard during each contraction. I thought I'd have a difficult time getting the right leverage to slug Al if I was standing up.

The birth center also wanted to know how many people were planning to attend, what our video needs would be, and whether we required space in the refrigerator for casseroles. This threw me for a loop, since the experience was starting to sound more like a catered bar mitzvah than a natural physical event. I didn't really want anyone at the birth—frankly, I wished that I didn't have to be there, either. And I certainly didn't want pictures taken until after our child had left my body.

So far, developing the plan had seemed odd. But then on one of the last visits the midwife hit us with the weirdest non-option of all. "I'm obliged to let you know that you will be disposing of your own placenta," she said, producing a document for us to sign.

Alan and I looked at each other in panic. She then explained that hospitals sell their old placentas to special placenta-retrieval services, but that the birth center didn't have enough to sell each month. So it was the clients' responsibility to dispose of it as they saw fit. Some people buried it under a tree, for example, she said.

"I think you should drive out of there and stash it in the nearest dumpster at some fast food restaurant," said my friend Sandy when I told her about it.

Before this, Al and I had never really thought about the placenta at all. But knowing that it was coming home with us, we started to imbue it with a personality. We began seeing it as an evil twin of the baby we were about to have, and sifted through our list of rejected baby names to see what we would call it. We gave it Alan's last name, since we had decided that our daughter would have mine.

In the end, some of the options we picked worked out pretty well. I did try Jacuzzi labor and liked it, even though they made me leave the tub to actually give birth. Getting me out of the hot water must have been difficult, since apparently I was thrashing around and yelling at Al, "Pull me out of this Jacuzzi and you're a dead man."

My mother contributed to the birthing experience by baking a nice casserole, and even decided to be in the room as K was born.

Leaving to go home the next day, proudly clutching our new bundle of joy, we were taken aback as the nurse handed us what felt like a pound and a half of chopped meat wrapped in brown butcher's paper.

Yep, it was Placenta, whom we had forgotten all about in the excitement of our daughter's birth. And now it was ours forever, or at least until we decided what to do with it. At least we didn't need a separate car seat or snowsuit for it. We weren't living at home at the time (my remodeling illness had forced us to move temporarily to an apartment), so it would be impossible to bury Placenta in the backyard. And I had grown too attached to it to go the fast food disposal route. So the only thing we could figure out to do was to take it home and freeze it.

I recommend this course of action, in case you ever have a placenta disposal problem. It gave Al something to do when people came to see the new baby—he could take the guys into the kitchen and show them the placenta in the freezer next to the Häagen-Dazs. The only problem was, when it came to actually burying the thing when we got back to our own house, we didn't know the proper procedure. Should we defrost it first in the microwave, or bury it still frozen?

We decided on the latter, and Al buried Placenta under a hydrangea bush about two months after our kid's birth. It was a simple ceremony.

Cathy Crimmins is a prolific humorist from the Philadelphia area.

41

What They Don't Teach You in Childbirth Class

April Burk

In childbirth classes it's important to cover stages of labor, breathing techniques, what a newborn really looks like, etc. But what about the other things they really should tell you?

If you're modest, get over it.

The deterioration of my modesty began during labor when at least three students popped in to ask if they could observe. Looking at them framed between the "V" of my widespread legs, I couldn't quite get out the words, "What more could you possibly want to see?" between contractions, so the midwife gently but firmly told them no. It didn't matter that we had specified "no observers" on our birth plan, nor that we reaffirmed this decision when we pre-registered. Perhaps packing a door-sized "No Trespassing" poster in my birth bag would have helped preserve my modesty, but not for long. Soon after delivery, a breastfeeding consultant came in, and without so much as mentioning the weather, squeezed my nipples and manipulated my breasts to show me correct nursing techniques. Until this happened, I had no idea how embarrassed I could feel.

The tape goes in back.

In the hospital the next day, I tentatively dressed the squirming new member of our family for departure. The pediatrician came in to do one last checkup and asked, "Who changed her diaper?" I proudly raised my hand. "It's on backwards," he scowled. "The tape goes in back, the dancing bears go in front." I felt so stupid that I half expected bars to clamp down over all the exits and alarms to shrill, preventing our escape with this vulnerable life. When the hospital doors opened, I jumped in the car with the baby and yelled at my husband, "Go, go, go!" I watched the rearview mirror all the way home, but no one made me stop and give my daughter back.

Any shred of remaining modesty will evaporate.

Finally in the privacy of my own home, I settled down to begin the business of bringing up baby. During that third-week growth spurt, Kayla wanted to eat every fifteen minutes. My pull-up shirts were damp with milk stains, and my fingers had formed calluses from buttoning and unbuttoning my tuck-in blouses. Finally, I just tossed my shirt and bra in the corner so baby had instant access to her food supply. At this point, I couldn't have cared less if the entire Mormon Tabernacle Choir saw me.

After Kayla got through her growth spurt, I started wearing clothes again and we were able to venture out for short excursions. During a stroll through the mall, I noticed an elderly lady staring at my chest in a persnickety way. Had I left my shirt unbuttoned again? I looked down and saw my hands matter-of-factly cupping and lifting my breasts, weighing them to judge which side to offer first at feeding time. Oh geez, how long had I been doing that?

Keep your algebra book handy and other advice.

Between all that breathing practice in class, there are some sage tidbits that occasionally filter through. Among these is "sleep when the baby sleeps." This is critical because your baby sure won't sleep when you do. When you see that little head nod, do whatever you have to. Take the phone off the hook, unplug the doorbell, read your high school algebra book—just knock yourself out. Even if you have to sit up in a chair with baby and front carrier still attached. Go to sleep!

But remember, when you wake up, the baby's not the only one who will be hungry. Since you'll be in no mood to prepare a five-course dinner, be sure to accept all offers of casseroles from friends, relatives, or passing strangers. It's irrelevant if you sense the offer is insincere. Take it anyway. And if you want to keep visits with these well-wishers brief, follow these steps:

Before answering the door, put on a robe (even if you're dressed underneath) and muss your hair. Stifle a yawn from time to time, but don't stop your head from falling on your chest occasionally. If this is too subtle, tell your guests you're sorry they can't stay longer but the bags under your eyes are making you dizzy.

Learn how to be ambidextrous. Now.

Kayla always knew when I was ready to eat. It didn't matter if she had nursed two hours ago or within the last five minutes; she was hungry anytime I even looked at a plate of food. And it never failed that it was always time to feed her from my right side, leaving only my clumsy left hand free to maneuver a fork. If you find yourself in the same situation, here's a safety tip: make sure none of your meals are hot, because you will drop some on the baby, not that you remember what hot food tastes like anymore.

Remember that hands are not your only tools. Feet can move things from one room to another; toes can pick up dropped pacifiers and dirty socks. If you begin practicing now, you will soon be able to separate eggs with your left hand while applying mascara with your toes.

There's more.

There's more, lots more, but I have to feed the baby now. If you are even considering expanding your family, start practicing these new skills now. Breathing exercises and Kegels are important, too, but they pale in comparison to the lessons I've shared here. After all, labor will be over in a day or so, but some of this advice will be useful for a lifetime. Well, for a week anyway.

April Burk lives in Archer, Florida, with her family. Her work is included in Mother Voices *(Sourcebooks),* Forks in the Road *(Reiman Publications), and* A Fifth Portion of Chicken Soup for the Soul *(HCI).*

The Nursing Section

Your baby adores your breasts like
no lover ever will. Your partner
claims to love your breasts? Hah!
Did he ever cry all the way home
from the grocery store because he
couldn't hold onto one?

—*Barbara Kerley*

Lactation's Lament

Joan Scoggin

Oh, pain so fearsome,
Burdensome love, a mother
Does endure for one small babe
On nursing strike with dimpled
Smile and nary appetite.

Cannot find my feet so far
'Thout sighting down my armpit fair,
And recognize them only just
Past Partonesqued cursed 'zooms.

Have not stood straight like
Mighty oak in endless hazy hours,
Nor felt light touch of babe's
Dear pater without a shrinking fear.

Lactation's Lament

A squint develops, a list to the fore,
A low moan issues forth. But, oh, 'twas
Not a moan, but "moo!" Alack, 'tis
Gone too far!

My fevered brow is more than dewed,
'Tis running like a stream. No shirt
Does fit, and underthings are torturous
Garments indeed.

Unless you wake with thirst to slake,
My beauteous tiny one, mayhap thy mum
Will mere' explode, leaving puddles
In her wake.

Joan Scoggin is a mother of three of her own children and also mothers nearly anyone else under the age of 50 who dares to cross her threshold. Living far enough into the heartland to actually have had a real prairie chicken in her yard, she and her wonderfully tolerant husband have been married seventeen years, which they both attribute to their silly senses of humor.

The Nursing Section for Me, Please

Roz Warren

I try to be discreet. It's not as if I stand up in the middle of a crowded restaurant, haul out a tit, and shout, "HEY EVERY-BODY LOOK AT ME!" Instead, I quietly unsnap my coveralls and unobtrusively slip the baby in under my T-shirt. You'd barely know what I was up to. Yet, some people glare at me as if I'm sitting there mainlining hard drugs instead of nurturing my young. When I get one of their outraged looks I want to ask, "What the hell do you think breasts are for?" But I already know the answer—women have breasts to titillate men. I'm exposing my breasts to turn on guys!

Nursing my baby is just an excuse; I probably only had the kid so I could display my fabulously exciting milk-filled tits in restaurants and airports, right? Still, the nasty looks inform me in no uncertain terms that I'm breaking the rules. I'm not sup-posed to uncover my breasts in public to feed my hungry baby. I'm supposed to uncover them in some guy's bedroom to drive him wild with lust.

The Nursing Section for Me, Please

The looks I get from men are bad enough, but what can you expect? It's when women glare at me that I feel betrayed. Mostly older women, but plenty of younger ones too. The message seems to be that nursing is a vulgar and unsightly practice to be hidden away from the eyes of decent people. Look—if you don't like what you see, you've got a neck. Turn your head. I'll be damned if I'm going to skulk off to the bathroom to sit on the toilet or floor, breathing the twin aromas of stale cigarette smoke and Tidy bowl as I feed my baby to the pulsating rhythm of flushing johns. Would you want to eat dinner in a public restroom? My baby doesn't either.

It's not as if a comfortable or even remotely suitable place is ever provided for nursing in private. A bathroom with a chair at all—let alone a comfortable one—is as rare as a businessman in a three piece suit who approaches you and says, "A nursing mother—what a beautiful sight!" Nursing in the bathroom usually means sitting on the floor with the cigarette butts, as other women come in and out and comment on your condition. Blank stares are the norm. The occasional expressions of support and outrage—"What a shame you have to hide away in here to feed your baby!"—are as infrequent as they are appreciated.

Maybe in addition to having "Smoking" and "No Smoking" sections, public places can have "Nursing" and "No Nursing" sections. Then the grumps and grouches can be spared the awful sight of those of us who need to get on with the crucial task of childrearing.

A friend of mine was paid a visit by her grandmother, who came by to see her great-grandchild for the first time. The baby got hungry; Karen proceeded to nurse him. Grandma was shocked. "Doesn't it bother you to nurse in public?" she asked (referring, of course, to Karen's own living room). "Oh no," said Karen. "I love to nurse in public! When there aren't enough people around here I bundle up the baby and take him out to the airport to nurse!"

That's the right attitude.

Roz Warren is a radical feminist mom and editor of many women's humor books, including Women's Lip *(Sourcebooks) and* Men are from Detroit, Women are from Paris *(Sourcebooks).*

Lactation Obfuscation

Carol Delaney

During the years in a woman's life when she chooses to allow her reproductive organs to function, the rest of her culture chooses to avert its eyes. Since during this time a woman's emotions and instincts are residing in some other culture, her intellect must compensate so that she may hold her place in contemporary society. This compensation includes allowing no sign that her breasts are lactating for her baby. Some tips to maintain this ludicrous façade follow.

Language can be used to soothe both men and women who find this particular use of breasts distasteful. Remember that you are not breastfeeding your baby: you are nursing.

It is possible to breastfeed a baby by lifting a shirt from the waist and unhitching the nursing bra with one hand. No one will see your breast—not even the baby, who latches on in a flash and is covered by the then dropped shirt. Everyone is protected from the spectacle of a misappropriated sexual object.

In the early weeks of breastfeeding, your breasts will be large and firm. Although during this time your libido is vacationing in Antarctica, your breasts are more attractive than they have ever been. If you are the cultural victim most of us are, your self-esteem will jump.

Then comes the crash. Breasts soften and sag due to the changes of pregnancy, not breastfeeding, but breastfeeding is continually blamed. Now you must invest in a sturdy, support-ive brassiere to maintain the illusion of the breasts of a twenty-year-old maiden. This is the size and shape designed into the fashions we have to choose from.

Body fluids are most unattractive. So don't let leaking milk show! Bras must be stuffed with cotton pads and changed when wet so no person can see that you are using your breasts to feed your baby. Rarely will your breasts leak much milk after the first few months, so you won't have this culturally imposed stress for long.

Subjects to be shared only with carefully chosen, sounded-out peers: breastfeeding baby past the age of one; breastfeeding while pregnant; breastfeeding siblings of different ages at the same time; your child's fondness for your breasts after breast-feeding has ended; that utter lack of interest in sex with your partner mentioned above. All of these pass; all fall within the normal course of breastfeeding. None are among the experiences allotted an alluring modern female.

Health professionals, health researchers, and even formula manufacturers encourage women to breastfeed their babies, but they all wish us to conform to these peculiar rituals of propriety while feeding our babies. Breastfeeding is a glorious element of our sexuality. By seeing through the culturally imposed restrictions, it can be especially fulfilling, pleasurable, and feminine.

Carol Delaney breastfed a few babies—all her own—through many, many years in which she also led an active social life and endured brief encounters with the workplace.

Ask Dr. Baby

Never allow your child to call
you by your first name. He hasn't
known you long enough.

—*Fran Lebowitz*

Night-Owl

Janet Ruth Heller

Midnight footsteps
Advancing
Yet closer.
A knock.

Finally,
"Ma-ma!"
Jamie enters,
Diapers soaked.

Janet Ruth Heller is an assistant professor of English at Albion College in Michigan. She is a founding mother and editor of Primavera, a women's literary magazine. Her book of literary criticism was published by the University of Missouri Press and her poetry has been widely published.

Ask Dr. Baby

Alison J. Conte

If only babies would tell us what they want. A simple, "No, thank you," would be so much easier than scrubbing spinach off the floor. Unfortunately, by the time they are able to talk, we've forgotten what the question was.

At last, here are answers to your questions from the expert with the correct point of view.

Dear Dr. Baby:

When I stop my baby girl from drawing in my checkbook or scattering three hundred paper napkins around the room, she screams in frustration and throws herself on the floor passionately sobbing. Why does she react so violently?

What would you do if you were engrossed in a fascinating hobby and a nine-foot-tall giant picked you up and dragged you away? Or, if someone shut off the TV in the middle of a football game? Wouldn't you resent it? Life is constant frustration for us babies.

You big guys make up the rules and always win. How about a game that I can win for a change? Like, "How fast can you pull all the silverware off the table?"

Dear Dr. Baby:
Jennifer babbles and babbles. What do these sounds mean?

Do you think you sound any clearer to her?

Dear Dr. Baby:
Andy is almost one. Why does he rip up every newspaper, catalog, and book in the house?

Ripping is the most interesting thing that can be done to paper. We babies don't read and your books have no pictures. Ripping makes a great sound and we create two pieces where there was only one! By ripping some more we can create a paper snowstorm and change the way the whole carpet looks.

Dear Dr. Baby:
My son, Justin, just learned to walk. Now he wants to climb, usually onto the dining room table. Why?

If you'd been looking at kneecaps for a year, wouldn't you want the best view you could get?

Dear Dr. Baby:
Why does my son feed the dog his food?

Dogs and babies have a Bill of Rights all their own. Babies feed the dog any food that they can sneak off the plate. Dogs know this and make it as easy as possible for the child, hanging around the high chair where food usually falls. When we see you feed Daisy a dog biscuit, we naturally think you are sharing your cookies with her.

Dear Dr. Baby:
Why does my child yell and scream for no reason? She's not upset, she's just loud.

This is an area where we may never meet. Babies love to scream. It sounds great and it reminds us of when crying brought food, love, and comfort. Another benefit of screaming is that it brings adult activity to a halt. Sometimes we just want to join in the conversation. But basically, screaming is just fun. Try it sometime.

Dear Dr. Baby:
Why does my two-year-old constantly interrupt when I'm talking to someone?

Why not? Adults are boring. They sit around doing nothing but talk for hours at a time. We are simply trying to get you out of this rut and into something more interesting. Like pouring juice on the floor or fingerpainting the cat.

Dear Dr. Baby:
My fifteen-month-old son loves to mash and splash his food, but he's not very interested in eating. How come?

Grown-ups mash and splash their food all the time, except you call it slicing and stirring. He's simply an inept imitator. You also eat with your fingers, which for some reason is OK with french fries but not with mashed potatoes. Soup, by the way, is just a small bowl of bathwater, and everyone knows that baths are for getting wet. Feed us soup and accept the consequences.

Dear Dr. Baby:
I'm trying to teach my daughter to eat. How come she can put everything into her mouth—lint, buttons, bugs, paper— except the spoon?

Once she's tasted the hard, flavorless spoon, the mystery is gone. Bugs are crunchy. Paper gets wet. These are worthy of further mouth exploration. Besides, food slides off the spoon. It is obviously a rhythm instrument, best banged on the bowl. Food is to be eaten with the hands, where it can be squished through the fingers for maximum tactile sensation.

Dear Dr. Baby:

When my baby Andrea and I are at the mall, she walks in any direction as long as it's not the one I'm going in. How come?

Maybe she knows about a private sale. Actually, it's a strike out for freedom. You see, babies are slaves, captive by our need for food and protection. Besides, we can't drive. But even small freedoms, like walking where we want to, give a feeling of independence. You come running after us and we achieve the ultimate goal, power.

Alison Conte enjoys gardening, traveling, cooking, writing, and astronomy. She lives with her daughter, husband, and their Manchester Terrier in Sewickley, Pennsylvania.

Truth and the Consequences

Donna Black

I'm constantly amazed how many other names are used when referring to certain body parts. Especially when dealing with children. For example, we were eating dinner with another family at a local restaurant when little Lisa turned to her mom and stated, "Mommy, my she-she needs to go wee-wee." And with the usual chain reaction, her brother piped right in with, "Daddy, my he-he needs to go pee-pee." Fortunately, because my two girls had no idea what their friends were talking about, I got to skip the adventure of taking toddlers to a foreign bathroom. On another occasion, while playing at the park, I actually heard a man say to his son who was holding his crotch, "Hey, Tim, my man, do ya need to go drain your tool (grunt, grunt)?" I mean, come on—his "tool"?

She-she, he-he, and tool? Nope, I decided that when my girls were old enough to ask, they would simply be told the real names of the body part and body function in question. So, when my three-and-a-half-year-old pointed below her waist and asked why water came out, I explained that the "water" came out of her urethra and was called urine and to please not drink it or try to get her little sister to drink it. And when she happened to see her dad using the bathroom and asked what that "thing" was and why he stood up, I simply told her that "thing" was a penis and that's what men and boys use to urinate (and to please not ever grab it like a rope to swing from it ever again!)

For awhile, she'd say, "Daddy has a peanut," and, not wanting to have my child accidentally create yet another ridiculous slang word for "penis" (not to mention my husband's embarrassment over being called the man with the peanut), I spent quite a bit of time getting her to pronounce "penis" correctly.

Alas, sometimes complete honesty can backfire, and even though I'm still a firm believer in teaching kids the real words for any body part and its function, I'm quite sure our straight talk was not appreciated during our most recent journey to Hot Springs Village, Arkansas.

Usually we go there to visit relatives; this time the trip was due to the death of Uncle Tom. We hadn't wanted to bring the kids but Aunt Betty insisted that they would be "rays of sunshine" during an otherwise somber event. It seemed Aunt Betty was right, too—all of the people we met (90 percent were over the age of seventy) seemed to enjoy watching the antics of our two little girls. And even during the memorial service, the girls behaved admirably. In fact, by the time the service was over, I was in the blissful and euphoric state of knowing I had two of the best little girls in the world.

Then came the dinner following the memorial service. Because everyone just loved our little darlings (my youngest was blowing kisses to everyone, which was so cute), the table we chose quickly filled with grandmas, grandpas, and great-grandparents eagerly wanting to spend more time with our two kids, who probably reminded them of their own grandchildren and great-grandchildren.

So there we all were, my husband and I beaming with pride over our perfect children, waiting to hear what lovable statements the two little angels would make. Well, the oldest angel decided not to waste this moment in the spotlight and with a glance around the entire table, she took a deep breath, began pointing to each of our tablemates while saying clearly and loudly (oh, so clearly and loudly), "You have a penis, and you have a vagina, and you have a penis, and...," until all the vaginas and penises at our table had been addressed.

I had never before seen the "domino effect" of mouths dropping open in shock and, quite frankly, I hope never to again. All I could think during those moments of great trial and tribulation (with my husband muttering, "You just had to teach her to say penis correctly, didn't you...") was that at least my littlest angel hadn't let me down. As I bent my head to kiss her silky soft blond halo, I couldn't help but notice—as did everyone else—that she was quite busy with her finger up her nose.

Donna Black is a writer from Texas.

The Family Dinner Hour

Ask your child what he wants
for dinner only if he's buying.

—*Fran Lebowitz*

The McSecret

Lauren Andreano

If you promise not to tell, I'm going to let you in on Mother's Little Secret. This secret may shock the intelligent, socially responsible mother of the '90s. It's politically incorrect, crass, commercial, and downright hazardous to your health, but it can give you a precious hour of semi-peace and quiet, and keep you out of the kitchen for the night. It's McDonald's. Or Burger King, or Jack-in-the-Box, or any of those fast food places whose flashy advertising leaves you explaining to a five-year-old about high blood pressure, rainforests, and how tofu and lima beans can be just as exciting when molded into cute little shapes.

Fast food has always been taboo for our children; we are a "the-body-is-a-temple" kind of family. This healthy living is my husband's idea; I was a "Devil-Dog-and-coffee-for-breakfast" kind of gal before we shared a kitchen table. But we vowed to raise nutritionally correct children. Nothing but whole wheat loaves in our bread box. Fruit Loops and Cocoa Puffs are out, Bran Flakes and Puffed Rice are in. Dessert is yogurt sprinkled with wheat germ. The thought of our little ones ingesting a candy bar would make us reach for the number of the Poison Control Hotline.

So it was a fluke that I would discover this secret. The kids and I were driving home tired and grouchy from a long day of errands and activities. I did not look forward to dinner. My husband was on a business trip, being wined and dined at an exclusive steak house in Chicago. My whining and dining experience, I knew, would involve convincing the kids to eat their peas. Then I spotted it—a Burger King! Perhaps jealousy made me turn into that driveway, file the kids into a place decorated with orange plastic, and urge them to order grease in the form of meat and potatoes.

We sat in the relative quiet. I sipped my coffee, hummed with the Muzak, and observed my kids so caught up in dunking the usually forbidden chicken chunks in ketchup and slurping their sodas that they forgot to fight. "This is good," I sighed contentedly to myself, somewhat surprised. And it was.

Since that momentous day, I have perfected fast food suppers into an art that you, too, can appreciate, if you follow my personally researched guidelines.

- Don't go with a health-conscious person. It is impossible to enjoy the secret sauce on a burger while your dining partner reads the fat content from the federally mandated nutritional information found near the bathrooms.

- Timing is everything. Avoid the after-soccer crowd, which is especially rowdy and sweaty, and Saturdays, when the place is packed with divorced Dads who can't figure out what else to do with the kids. Do not go on Friday nights, when every other stressed out, fed up parent brings the family and the place is wound up tighter than a jack-in-the-box ready to spring. At all costs avoid senior citizen night, when you are assured a lot of dirty looks from people who don't remember that even nice kids blow bubbles in their sodas.

- Choose an establishment that does not have one of those annoying playlands. Quiet enjoyment is impossible amid screams for Angela to stop throwing plastic balls at the McCashier, or for Jason to keep his head away from the bottom of the McSlide.

- Don't hold out the promise of fast food as a reward for good behavior. Your kids may disappoint you by acting in their usual manner, leaving you to cancel your kitchen-free evening and do the Shake 'n' Bake thing.

- Have no deadline. Fast food refers to how they prepare it, not how a three-year-old eats it. It's easy to watch your child dawdle over his hamburger, make stick people with his french fries, and push his new toy Batmobile up and down the plastic table for an hour if you've got no place to go and the coffee refills are free.
- Fast food should always be the kids' forbidden fruit, the ultimate indulgence. Don't spoil the mood by going too often. And do allow their father to constantly lecture them on the evils of a McBLT.
- Above all, don't let on that you enjoy it.

Take my advice. Abandon your principles and discover the secret pleasures of fast food. You're smiling—have you already discovered it? You mean, you were going to keep this a secret from me?

Lauren Andreano is a writer and humorist living in Pennsylvania.

In Celebration of the Family Dinner Hour

Joan Scoggin

Sociologists have recently expressed their concern that American families are neglecting that ritual bonding ceremony known as the dinner hour. These same students of family life tell us that the dinner hour is a time for expressing differing viewpoints, engaging in serious or lighthearted discussions, making group decisions, and generally reaffirming our dedication to one another. For those same people, I'd like to offer up the following example of how my family has taken the importance of the dinner hour to heart, and all the many wonderful experiences it has brought to our lives. Picture, if you will...

The oldest child, a six-year-old boy, is raising holy hell about how his chicken is "empty." None of the rest of us is entirely sure what that means, but it doesn't matter because he is making a jarring conversational transition to earnestly pleading for an entire box of Corn Pops to be given to him in a family-sized serving dish, and swears by all that is sacred that he WILL eat the entire thing.

Somehow, this prompts him to pick up the salad tongs and wave them at his sister, threatening that "she'd better not say she wants Corn Pops too!" His four-year-old sister reacts by doing her "little girl at three G's" face and pasting herself against the chairback. As soon as he looks away, she pours a good spoonful of corn down the back of his shirt.

Meanwhile, our twenty-two-month-old baby is very, very carefully separating his food into bite-sized pieces and dropping it on the dog's head to see what critical mass must be achieved before the dog notices that her own head smells mighty tasty. My husband is seated opposite me, and he fixes me with a glare indicating that it was entirely unnecessary for me to spend so much time training the children to do all this just special for him.

I, thinking to add a little levity to the situation, have not yet learned the value of silence, and suggest to the children that we sing grace, and add in the line we use at lunch about "thank you God for these wriggly children with their smelly feet," which gives my husband apoplexy, and he loses the ability to speak coherently.

He begins uttering spurts of near-language that seem to add up to a desire not to say anything about feet during grace, but, unfortunately, it's way too late because the rest of us are in full voice and have moved on to the line about "scraped up knees and sunshine smiles" in a melody that sounds suspiciously like "Farmer in the Dell."

The baby, gleeful at our family's melodic expression of thanks, has grasped his spoon in one hand and is heartily beating it against his highchair tray in syncopated time with the tune, and with his other hand is pointing directly at his father, and he is clearly enunciating, "NAR!" repeatedly.

I don't serve soup at dinner anymore because I think that watching their father drown himself in chicken noodle might traumatize the children, but perhaps I ought to check back with some of the sociologists on that point.

Joan Scoggin is a mother of three of her own children and also mothers nearly anyone else under the age of 50 who dares to cross her threshold. Living far enough into the heartland to actually have had a real prairie chicken in her yard, she and her wonderfully tolerant husband have been married seventeen years, which they both attribute to their silly senses of humor.

A Child's Garden of Delights

Sally Curd

A Child's Garden of Delights, a new restaurant especially for children, opened in our area last month. It is a lovely addition to this fast-growing trend of specialty restaurants.

Our first visit to A Child's Garden of Delights was quite pleasant. The vinyl washable wallpaper, featuring life-sized drawings of The Simpsons, Batman, and Kevin Costner as Robin Hood, immediately energizes the incoming patrons waiting in the lovely foyer. We were offered complimentary aperitifs of Swiss Miss and Thirstbuster while the children took advantage of the swing set, a teeter-totter, and a sand box with pails and shovels. Of course, the eight-week-old kittens playing in the sandbox do sometimes lead to problems, but when you are being escorted to your table by Big Bird or Oscar the Grouch, these things are quickly forgotten.

Our waitress, dressed as Little Bo Peep, quickly appeared at our table. "Hi! My name is Carol," she chirped. "I'll be your waitress tonight, and I'll also be your waitress if you come back again next Wednesday; but don't come on Thursday, or I won't be here. I was born in Ventura, California. I went to high school in Santa Clara, and had a 3.5 grade point average. My favorite color is blue. I wear a size seven junior petite. I am pinned to a Kappa Sigma from UCLA. I have three brothers and four sisters. My parents met at an Encounter Group in Sausalito in 1969. I have had a year at San Diego State. I want to get married in 4 years and have 3.2 children. My favorite food is french fries. Only don't get them here. They're grody to the max. I will be serving you 'til 12:30 when Katie comes on duty to serve your needs. Unless Katie is sick tonight—she wanted to go out with her boyfriend. In that case, Susan will be your waitress. She was born in Woodstock, New York..."

Carol stopped to catch her breath again. Seizing the moment, we grabbed the menus. (The charming menus feature the Pop-Up Book format, and are written in the Look-Say Method for children who have a sight vocabulary of only one hundred words. These are replacing the menus using Phonics Approach, which only last month promised to abolish illiteracy but have since been found to be educationally unsound, racist, and linked to regressive toilet training.)

The luncheon special that day was the Peanut Butter and Jelly Sandwich with Ruffled Potato Chips and Root Beer. The sandwich was the best I've ever tasted, and should end, once and for all, the controversy over the properly made peanut butter and jelly sandwich. Garden of Delights is definitely of the Mixed School. That is, the peanut butter and jelly are vigorously mixed together rather than being spread on separate slices of bread as found in some inferior establishments. The bread, Balloon White, was fresh and totally without substance, bringing cheers from the two five-year-olds dining with us.

The root beer was served in frosted mugs, allowing for the fruity, complex fragrance to be fully appreciated. Garden of Delights' own root beer has a good nose, a hearty essence, and is well-aged in their own vats. (Tours of the Giant Root Beer Machine Room and the root vineyards are available on national holidays and can be scheduled by telephone. Ask for the beverage steward.) Extra wide straws are served with the root beer to facilitate blowing bubbles in the glass, as our two young diners demonstrated.

As a main course beverage, we chose the Pepsi Lite, an aromatic, substantial drink with a delicate balance. The Pepsi Lite had a charming flowery taste, but maintained a definable, pleasant backbone. It boasted a distinct varietal character and was highlighted with a subtle fruity essence. Other Pepsis have been disappointing, for they can be harsh and aggressive if opened too early. My companion commented that it was probably a 1994.

I Killed June Cleaver

"Surely not," I countered. "1997 was an excellent year for this varietal."

At any rate it was delightful to experience the engaging bouquet of a mature Pepsi Lite. It is available by the glass or carafe.

My companion ordered à la carte, choosing the Kraft Macaroni and Cheese Box dinner, while I ordered the Microwave Pizza with a Side of Onion Rings. While we waited for our orders to arrive, an appetizer tray, consisting of caramel corn, M&Ms, and Cheetos was brought to our table. These were enthusiastically consumed by all. The caramel corn was particularly outstanding—crunchy and sweet, in a lavender color. I think the flavor was Daiquiri Grape, but I am unsure, as it can often be confused with the Pina Colada Berry.

The macaroni and cheese was done to perfection, the brassy gold of the food coloring being set off by an artificial parsley sprig and three green beans. The macaroni and cheese was served al dente, and the dish was well-presented on Garden of Delights' own plastic plates bearing various inscriptions, such as souvenir of the Grand Canyon or Holiday Inn.

My microwave pizza was less satisfactory; the two or three slices of pepperoni did not make up for the transparent layer of cheese food on the three-inch crust. Additionally, the pizza was rather chewy, as the children and my Significant Other were already on their desserts while I was still masticating.

The desserts were the hit of the meal. The hostess brought around a tempting selection: Jello Pudding Pops, Dairy Queen Blizzards, cotton candy, and S'mores. Wanting to sample everything, we were pleased with each of the offerings except the S'mores. They had a decidedly non-campfire taste, having been microwaved at the same time as the pizza.

The ambience of the Garden is enhanced by the other waiters, dressed as Ninja Turtles, Roseanne, or the Terminator, and by careful attention to other details to keep patrons in the spirit of dining with children. In the restrooms, plastic toys and miniature cars clutter the sinks.

Before his fall from grace, I understand that pictures of Pee Wee Herman graced the restrooms, but the management discreetly decided that, no matter what stance parents took on the Pee Wee Herman issue, the restrooms might not be the wisest place to put his picture. A more prudent choice, scenes from Mr. Rogers' Neighborhood, now can be found throughout the restaurant.

The service at the Garden is excellent. At the table next to us, demands for washcloths and bibs were quickly attended to, a sign that the Chocolate Perfection was a success with the two high chair infants who had most of it in their hair.

The daily luncheon specials provide the Garden with lots of variety so that children should never tire of the menu. In addition to the pizza and Peanut Butter and Jelly sandwiches, daily specials include Hot Dogs, Spaghetti-O's, Trix, and Muppet Baby Muffins.

While dining at the Garden, we recommend entering their giant prize giveaway drawing, announced monthly. First prize is an all-expense-paid trip to Disneyland. Second prize, an audio casette, "Madonna Reads Your Favorite Bedtime Stories," and third prize, a copy of the video *Home Alone*.

Many of the young diners were oblivious to the presence of adults because they were wearing the orange headphones provided by the restaurant and gyrating to the music of Thrasher as they munched their chicken nuggets and tater tots.

We can recommend A Child's Garden of Delights. It is certain to please children of all ages as well as their parents. On weekends (and other times when nap schedules are curtailed) reservations are advised.

Master Charge, Visa, Diner's Club accepted; tricycle & stroller access.

Sally Curd writes and lives in Tucson, Arizona.

Spit-Shining the Kids

Even when freshly washed
and relieved of all obvious
confections, children tend to
be sticky.

—*Fran Lebowitz*

Laundry Mom

Joan Scoggin

Yea, though I walk
through the valley of
grape juice, I shall fear
no stain. I carry borax,
vinegar, baking soda, and my
Shout stick. I am
LAUNDRY MOM.

Pit discolorations,
mysterious brownnesses on
pants' legs are no challenge
for my box of Biz.
Wielding a stain chart
the likes of which no
mortal man has seen, I
vanquish all visual unpleasantness
from the clothing of my

beloved family. I am
LAUNDRY MOM.

Blotches, blots, smears, smudges, and
blemishes surrender to my
superior knowledge and bleach
paste. Out, out damned spot; had
Lady MacBeth but had my
Kenmore, she, too, could have greeted
the morn with crisp, good-smelling
sheets,
and a pristine pair of
panties.

Alas, the quest for lustrous whites
has led to elastic fatigue, and,
woe, woe, woe,
my straps are sprung.
Weep a small tear, but only one,
for not even threats of unbalanced foreview
shall dissuade me from my pursuit, for
I am
LAUNDRY MOM.

Joan Scoggin is a mother of three of her own children and also mothers nearly anyone else under the age of 50 who dares to cross her threshold. Living far enough into the heartland to actually have had a real prairie chicken in her yard, she and her wonderfully tolerant husband have been married seventeen years, which they both attribute to their silly senses of humor.

Keeping 'Em Clean

Lynne Ewing Mayesh

Busy hands are happy hands, my mother used to say. When my children were younger, they seemed to agree. Whether it was washing the dishes, the dog, or the car, they wanted to help. Even their rooms looked tidy if you didn't peek under the beds. I can even remember one birthday when my daughter Amber asked for a toy broom set.

By the time the kids started junior high school, getting them to help around the house was a problem I could no longer sweep under the rug. I always thought chores helped children learn responsibility, but now Jonathan and Amber acted as if it was my way of getting even with them for my labor pains.

Then, one day, Jonathan ran home, holding up a dollar. "Look at this!" he yelled. A neighbor had paid him for raking up her leaves. The secret was out. Complete strangers would pay him for the same tasks I expected him to do for free. And I thought I had trouble before.

A week later, after shuffling through knee-deep leaves in

search of the morning paper, I asked, "What about the leaves at home?"

He handed me two dollars. "See if Jimmy down the street can do it. His rates are cheaper than mine."

"Maybe Jimmy would go clothes shopping with me, too," I threatened. "I bet his smaller sizes are also cheaper."

Jonathan easily spent more time telling me why he could not do a chore than it would ever take to do it.

"You could have made your bed in the amount of time you've spent arguing with me about it," I pointed out.

He looked at the clock. "You're right. Gotta catch the bus," he shouted and slammed out the door.

His bed remained a tangle of blankets and sheets, but it matched the mishmash of dirty clothes, books, and dried pizza crusts on his floor.

Once, after I had collected and washed the soiled jeans from his floor, I made the mistake of taking the clean clothes back to his room while he was in it.

"Don't step there," he shouted.

I looked down at the floor. It looked no different from the rest of the room—like a two day old rummage sale.

"My biology paper," he offered—as if I should have known.

The smudged paper beneath my uplifted foot was something he was turning in for a grade.

That explained a lot.

Then he saw the clean jeans in my hands.

"You didn't wash those jeans?"

"Why not?" I asked.

"They're my never wash ones. What will my friends say?"

"Put them out in the street and I'll drive over them," I answered.

Later when my neighbor came over to chat, she asked, "Do you know whose jeans those are lying out in the street?"

At least Jonathan kept his disorder in his room. Amber turned the house topsy-turvy and I was "Momster" for insisting she pick up her clutter. I would say something cruel like, "Get your wet bathing suit off the couch," and she would cry back, "Why do you always have to act like Attila the Mom?"

No other mother in town, perhaps the nation, cared if their children splashed Cokes on the floor, stopped up the sink with oatmeal face scrub, or tracked sand in from the beach.

"Diane's mother does dishes so Diane can do her homework," Amber smirked.

"You claim you never have any homework; maybe that's the problem," I suggested.

At a PTA meeting, I met Diane's mother. She pointed a finger at me. "I've heard all about you!"

Had Amber hung out our dirty linen for the neighbors to

see? I couldn't think of anything I'd done that was worth gossiping about, so why point a finger at me?

Then she continued, "Diane claims you do dishes so Amber can study. She also says you don't care if Amber spills coke, stops up the sink, or tracks in sand. She claims you're the perfect mother."

How did I respond to such accusations? I just smiled. It was nice to know there was a teenager someplace who didn't think I was all washed-up.

Lynne Ewing Mayesh is the author of Party Girl (Knopf). *She lives in Los Angeles and her two children are now grown. One is a molecular biologist; the other is a lawyer.*

Spit-Shining the Kids

Barbara A. Tyler

Either maternal instinct is a myth or mine is broken. This bothered me until I realized I didn't need it. This mystical instinct has nothing to do with recognizing my children. (Mine are the ones that don't come when I call.) Instinct doesn't keep me from jabbing myself with diaper pins, and I'm learning to get the Hot Wheels out of the VCR through trial and error.

I'll admit, it would have been handy to have that instinct to help sort out the baby's cries. But I managed to figure it out on my own. If I feed him and he stops crying, it's a hungry cry. If he stops crying when I change him, it's a wet cry. If I feed and change him and he continues to cry, it's obvious—he wants Daddy.

Dealing with the older children is trickier. A little maternal instinct would be handy, but I can live without it. I have what every parent needs to survive: the Three Basic Parenting Reflexes.

1. Counting to three.

Just as Pavlov's dog learned to drool at the sound of a bell, I've learned to count at the sound of a fight. Although, there are days when I'm sure drooling would be just as effective.

For now, I'll stick with counting. So what if it doesn't work? Drooling looks bad. Besides, my children already think I'm an idiot because no matter how slowly I count, I never get higher than three. This must bother them a lot, because they're constantly trying to teach me.

The lesson begins with a fight. I know it's a fight, because play is never punctuated by high-pitched wails of, "Mom!"

"One," I shout. The children, pleased that I have remembered my cue, encourage me by kicking, punching, and biting each other.

Their actions say, "C'mon, Mom, don't give up. You can do it!"

"Two!" I pause, listening for more wailing, biting, and kicking. The encouragement continues.

"Atta girl, Mom! What comes next?"

On three, I launch in and pry them apart. The children exchange confused looks.

"Poor Mom. She was so close," the looks say.

"Yeah, I thought for sure she'd make it to four this time."

2. Spit-shining the kids.

I developed this reflex when I discovered that children attract dirt. I don't mean common everyday dirt, I mean Mystical Invisible Dirt.

This sneaky variety of dirt has impressive powers. It can't be seen under normal household lighting. Mystical Invisible Dirt only shows up under special lighting like those fluorescent bulbs at the grocery store. Occasionally, it can be seen by candlelight, but only in fancy restaurants.

Coupled with this amazing power of invisibility, Mystical Invisible Dirt defies removal. Soap and water have no effect on it. The children may look clean inside the house, yet, in stores, they look like they've been sucking on mudsicles. The only thing that will remove Mystical Invisible Dirt is spit on a tissue. During tissue shortages, I have resorted to licking a thumb and rubbing the little grubmeisters' faces.

3. Using the child's full name.

This works best if you can remember the child's full name in the midst of whatever the child is doing.

Most of the time, I get the names right. Even if I don't, we have an unspoken rule: if Mom looks at you, even if she stutters through a list of everyone in the house, she really means you.

When I was pregnant with my third child, a friend suggested an alternative.

"Name him Ezekial Zebadiah," she said.

"Why?" I asked.

"Look at it this way. With a name like that, a child has to be well behaved," she explained. "If your name was Ezekial Zebadiah, would you want your mother hollering out the back door at you?"

Of course, she was assuming I'd be able to remember it without looking at the birth certificate.

These reflexes may not seem like much, but I couldn't survive without them. Don't get me wrong, I'm not knocking instinct. I think instinct is great if you've got it. As a matter of fact, if any of those instinctive parents are out there, I'd appreciate it if you could come look inside my VCR. I think there's a Hot Wheel stuck inside, but my hand is so swollen from jabbing it with diaper pins, I can't quite reach it.

Barbara A. Tyler is a freelance writer and mother of three.

Cleanliness

Angela D. Conroy

If cleanliness is next to Godliness, we are in big trouble at our house. Surely this statement was meant to exclude little boys! When they were young I gave them a bath every day. They would splash and coo as I lathered them up and rinsed them off with warm water. I'd rub them down with baby lotion and snuggle them close. It was aromatic bliss! They were so warm and pink and clean. Boy, have things changed.

Now shower/bath time is a tug of war. It's not that they don't like water—they do. They have swimming relays in the tub—when they finish there's as much water on the floor as in the tub. They have pulled down the shower curtain numerous times playing Marco-Polo. They fill the tub to within a quarter of an inch of the top (it's better for diving this way) and they use up all the hot water.

But despite all their aquatic adventures, they still come out dirty! They walk dripping through the whole house before they begin drying off.

"Are you guys all finished now? You don't look very clean. Did you wash your hair and use the soap?"

"No. You never said to do that."

"Guys, get right back in there and wash your hair and use the soap."

"Mom! There's no hot water left. We'll freeze to death!"

"I'm sorry, but you need to wash your hair and use the soap."

"We're gonna get pneumonia!"

"Go!" I holler back.

I should have realized that they had developed this indifference towards soap and shampoo when I cleaned their bathroom. A bottle of shampoo lasted so long that the packaging and the price had changed by the time I went to buy a new one. And the soap? It mildewed before it was used up. I have tried to impress upon them the importance of cleanliness. I don't mean compulsive cleanliness. I'm talking about bathing twice a week.

Once I picked up my three boys and three extras from the commons after a long hard day of play, and a friend of mine who has three little girls came over to the car to say "Hi." She stuck her head in the window and turned up her nose. "What's that smell?" she said.

"What smell?" I replied. "I don't smell anything."

"It smells like old tennis shoes in here."

"Oh, that. That's just the boys."

So if you ever see me hanging out in the "baby" aisle of the grocery store, sniffing the baby lotion—leave me in peace. I'm okay. I'm simply trying to keep an aromatic memory alive.

Angela D. Conroy is a happily re-married mom in a blended family with six children, four of whom are teenage boys. Needless to say, she is never at a loss for material about raising kids. She writes a monthly column for her community newspaper.

The Once-a-Month Housewife

Anne Hodge

A woman's life changes when she has children. When a baby is born, the new mother sheds not only some of the weight of pregnancy, she sheds also the rhythm of her life to date. Her life runs on a different cycle than before; a twenty-four-hour cycle, in which she is always busy but never seems to get anything done.

In her struggle to master this new timetable, the new mother may steal minutes from some more mundane or unnecessary tasks. She may stop wearing make-up. Stop styling her hair. Stop wearing clothes that need hand washing or ironing. Stop matching her earrings to her necklaces. Stop wearing earrings and necklaces.

Ceasing all these little operations does buy the mother more time, but none so much as curtailing housekeeping duties. Unfortunately, housekeeping is the one area where too much time parsimony can reflect badly on the housekeeper. Let's face it, a woman without make-up is only a woman without make-up, but a house without cleaning is a hovel. Does mother then have to pop the baby in his crib so she can scrub the kitchen floor? Is she obliged to let the television mind the children while she dusts each Venetian blind slat? Must she neglect her toddler to wash down the woodwork?

Many books have been written about streamlining housework, some of them even by mothers. Most of them even have good things to say. But the new mother (or the old mother, for that matter) is not interested in turning mattresses or cleaning the grille of the dishwasher with a toothbrush. She doesn't want to read an entire chapter about stain removal on furniture when she has already discovered that a strategically placed pillow or afghan eliminates a stain in a fraction of the time. She is looking for something quick, easy, and effective. She needs a mantra, and this is it: Wipe it off! Throw it out! Suck it up!

"Wipe it off!" refers to the wet cloth with which one dusts all surfaces both vertical and horizontal. (The only exception being antique wood surfaces for which a dry cloth will have to suffice.) Whether it's a sticky ring of orange juice, a dirty handprint, or a thin (or thick) layer of dust, the wet cloth will sweep it away and hold it until you can toss it into the washing machine where it will reemerge as those cute little wet felty balls to be popped into the trash.

"Throw it out!" sounds like cheating when in fact it is the most sensible of the affirmations. Look at all the one-legged Lego men. All those kiddie meal toys, and the single socks that have never found their mates. What will you really do with the stretched-out-of-shape hair elastics and the deck of 48 cards? Throw them away, I say, no more to clutter the home. Now, a conscientious mother may worry that she will toss out something important to her children like, say, a rock from the park where Billy's birthday party was. A few tossed out treasures will most likely encourage the younger family members (who may have been reminded nicely once or twice to pick up their things) to keep their possessions in a tidy manner. Or, everything of dubious value can be placed in a bag to be stored in the basement for easy retrieval. Or easy disposal.

"Suck it up!" is the final part of the hurried housekeeper's three-pronged attack on grime in the home. This refers, of course, to the use of a vacuum cleaner, not a straw. Creative use of this last step can actually eliminate the first two as most cleaners come with dusting attachments, and also do a good job of eliminating small broken toy parts, and gumball machine rings. The noise of the cleaner has the added benefit of shutting out cries for more juice, and phone calls from telemarketers, thereby making the time you have allotted for housework even more productive.

So, despite the fact that Mother pawed through her pile of unironed linen pantsuits to don the sweatsuit with the spit-up stains on the shoulder, and has her hair pulled back in the rubberband from the morning's paper, she has managed to clean her house well enough that she would not feel embarrassed by the arrival of an unexpected visitor. Even more important, she has enough time to play trucks on the floor, or mix a batch of playdough. All is well for another month, and then the ritual repeats itself. Yes, I did say "month." The ease with which the dust balls float out from under beds at the end of a month's time, and the satisfaction of doing a job that really needs doing makes it all the more rewarding for a mother with no time to clean.

Anne Hodge lives in a spotless house in sunny upstate New York where she is pampered by her doting husband, three adorable children, and pets that don't shed. She spends her days knitting sweaters, eating bonbons, and thinking up stories.

It's Wednesday and I Don't Have Any Clean Underwear

Sherri Jones Rivers

Today, time management for busy women is really the "in" thing. I've read some of the books and they have some good ideas, but I've concluded that some of us just aren't meant to have it all together. I'm definitely one of those who marches to a different drummer.

Wednesday at 7 A.M. was not unlike the beginning of most of my mornings. I had just opened my eyes and trudged downstairs in mismatched scuffs, when I heard my son's voice. Leaning over the banister, dripping wet from his shower, he yelled downstairs, "It's Wednesday, and I don't have any clean underwear."

"Just go through the hamper and find your least dirty pair," I suggested.

"Yuk," he said in disgust as he headed toward the bathroom.

I have my clothes-washing down to a science. I wash once a week, with the whites first in hot, then the permanent press on warm, and last, I do the towels and stuff on cold. A friend who is a home-economics major put me on to that idea. The only thing she didn't tell me was that you have to remember which day is wash day.

I stand in awe of friends who keep things in their households running smoothly. I have one friend, Janice, whose home looks like the cover of House Beautiful. One day I decided to drop by unexpectedly so as to catch something out of order. I made my way up the walkway. There were no pet-food dishes, bikes, roller skates, or pet frogs in the way. The door was disgustingly devoid of fingerprints. I rang the doorbell.

"Oh, hello," she said, checking her sculptured nails. "Please come in."

I followed her into the den. It had the faint markings of having just been vacuumed. All four children were sprawled on the floor, playing an educational card game.

"Excuse my mess," she said. "We've just gotten back from vacation and I haven't had time to get things straight."

I felt a severe case of envy coming on and went home sick.

I can never understand when a friend says, "My grocery day is Thursday." How can a person wait until Thursday? If I don't go to the store at least once a day, they call to see if I'm still alive. My husband says I'm the only woman he knows who goes to the grocery store every day, but still doesn't have anything in the house to eat.

It's bad enough that my husband realizes I'm disorganized, but I've been trying to hide it from the kids. All in vain.

Last night my son came home from a baby-sitting job, his eyes wide with excitement.

"Boy, do the Parkers have a shipshape house," he said. "Did you know that each kid has his own bathroom and they even have their names on their towels?"

I could tell he was impressed. "And that's not all," he continued. "When I opened their cabinets to get a snack, I saw the neatest thing. Mrs. Parker has her soups in alphabetical order."

"Well," I sighed. "I guess if she likes all the excitement taken out of her day, that's her business."

I was feeling really down when a neighbor called to invite me to a Ladies' Club meeting. "They're having the neatest speaker," she said. "She's from Homemakers Anonymous and she's going to speak on 'The Housewife's ABC's of Organization.' I thought you, of all people, might be interested."

"Thanks, Sue," I said. "But I'm afraid I'll have to decline. You see, it's Wednesday, and I don't have any clean underwear."

Sherri Jones Rivers is a freelance writer living in Augusta, Georgia. She presently is working with a publisher on a book of children's sermons.

Observations

Never have more children than
you have car windows.

—*Erma Bombeck*

Children's Car Pool Accord

Madeleine Begun Kane

Are you trapped behind the wheel of your family car? Do you feel more like a cabby than a mother and spouse? If so, a children's carpool may be precisely what you need. But be sure to work out a few details in advance. What details? Glad you asked. To preserve the peace in your neighborhood, all unsuspecting individuals involved should agree to the following before transporting a mob of marauding tots:

AGREEMENT entered into on [date], by five harried Mothers.

WHEREAS, herding children to and from school, ballet lessons, birthday parties, Gymboree, Little-League, play dates, scout meetings, and day camp completely monopolizes Mothers' lives;

WHEREAS, Mothers actually look forward to the day their kids can legally borrow the car keys;

WHEREAS, Mothers would like to have even half the social life enjoyed by their children, but lack the time or strength to do much more than collapse into bed;

NOW, THEREFORE, Mothers agree to the following car-pool guidelines:

1. Mothers shall take turns acting as the designated Driver on a daily rotational basis. They shall be well-insured and trained in the art of steering with two kids climbing on their shoulders and a third climbing over their laps.

2. Mothers' cars shall be fully equipped with seat belts, tissues, road maps, and first aid kits. Mothers affirm that they do not faint at the sight of blood, vomit, or melted chocolate seeping into their seats.

3. Drivers shall keep their back seats clear of breakables. In doing so, they shall keep in mind that a child can break anything.

4. Drivers shall not apply makeup while the car is moving, but may do so while waiting for a tardy child. However, Drivers shall have no legal recourse if squirming kids cause mascara mishaps.

5. If a Mother has an emergency on her driving duty day, she shall promptly notify the next Mother on the list. The following shall not be deemed emergencies:

a.　　A bad hair day.

b.　　A broken nail.

c.　　A headache. (Mothers always have a headache).

The cancelling Mother shall remain liable if her late notice results in the replacement Driver's arrest for indecent exposure.

7. Children shall be dressed, fed, and ready at the designated pick-up time. Moreover, they shall be free from contagious ailments and bladder overload.

8. If a child fails to emerge from his or her house within two minutes of Driver's arrival, Driver is authorized to honk. The delinquent child's Mother shall hold Driver harmless from any damage inflicted by infuriated neighbors.

9. Mothers shall make sure their children are equipped with all the appropriate items including, but not limited to, school books, lunch bags, leotards, swim suits, baseball gloves, batons, and sneakers. Each child shall be taught that the following words are banned: "I gotta go back to get my..."

10. Every Mother shall make reasonable efforts to notify the Driver that her child will not attend school or any other activity on any given day. Any Mother who strolls up to a waiting mommy-mobile and says, "Johnny doesn't feel like camp today," shall be required to take Johnny's place.

11. Each Mother represents that her child is angelically well-behaved. Mothers acknowledge that they are lying through their teeth.

12. Mothers shall caution their children not to disclose family secrets. Mothers promise to disbelieve everything they hear.

13. The following nutritional rules shall be strictly heeded:
a.   No candy, ice cream, or fast food detours.
b.   No eating or drinking in the car.
c.   Lunch boxes must be tightly secured—especially those bearing potato chips or overripe bananas.
14. No obscene language or gestures shall be permitted in any car. This includes the children.

15. The following events shall entitle the Driver to one month's freedom from driving duty.
a.   Arriving at a cancelled event with a car filled with kids.

b.   Bailing out a Mother who forgot it was her turn.

c.   Being saddled with a child whose Mother isn't home.

d.   A lunchbox–inflicted head wound.

e.   Anything involving the police.

16. The car radio shall be deemed the Driver's sole domain. So shall the steering wheel and pedals.

17. Each child who studies a musical instrument—especially the trumpet—shall be instructed not to play it in the car.

18. Mothers shall behave like mature adults at all times, no matter how severe the provocation. For example, Mothers shall never turn to a ten-year-old and say, "I've had it. You drive."

19. In order to minimize aspirin intake, Mothers shall instruct their darlings not to:

a.   Fistfight over window seats.

b.   Blow their nose on another child's shirt.

c.   Say, "Ha-ha. I can plié and you can't."

d.   Demonstrate twirling techniques in the car.

e.   Hang out the window at over 20 mph.

f.   Brag, "My mommy sold more cookies than your mommy."

g. Offer to show them hers if they will show her theirs.
h. Remove the cover from their science experiment.
i. Blow bubblegum bubbles within a foot of Driver's hair.
j. Use the cellular phone to order pizza.

20. Mothers acknowledge that there will be times when the kids are squirming, there's lots of screaming, and Driver's sure she's about to go berserk. During those challenging moments each Mother shall take comfort in this consoling thought: at least they're not in my house.

SIGNATURES: _____ _____ _____

_____ _____

Madeleine Begun Kane is a lawyer, oboist, and prolific writer. She is currently working on a collection of funny contracts.

Through the Bathroom Door

Angela D. Conroy

I am a big believer in sharing, and I spent countless hours explaining to my small sons the importance of sharing and the sense of bonding it could instill among family members. However, there are certain things I'd just as soon not share. And at the top of my list would be bathroom time. Now, as most of you moms out there know, this is not always an option when the kiddies are small. I myself hold some fond memories of myself and my three little chicks all crammed into one stall at the mall—one lounging on the floor visiting with our neighbors on either side, one trying to find out how many feet of toilet paper those gigantic rolls actually held, while the third one opened and shut the door.

And then there was bathtime. Whether they were in the tub or I was in the tub, we were all in the bathroom together. Ah yes, those were the days. Fortunately, as they grew older, they no longer wanted to be in the bathroom with me, but instead settled for the space right outside the door. Through the years

I have hardly missed a beat while on the other side of the bathroom door; spelling pre-tests, math facts drills, and proofreading essays. I signed permission slips and papers my kids slid under the door. I refereed disputes, pronounced judgments, and handed down punishments from the bathroom as well as shouted cheers, calmed fears, and dried tears all from the other side of the door. Naturally, each one of these tasks was urgent and required my immediate attention.

"Guys, I'm in the bathroom. Can't this wait?"

"No, Mom. I need it right now. Besides, you're not doing anything anyway."

"Good grief. Must I be busy every second? Fine. Slide it under the door."

So it should have come as no surprise that I managed to rent the only house on the mountain that had the master bath located directly in front of the turnstile that serves as my back door.

Now it became possible not only for me to visit with my own kids through the bathroom door, but anyone else who ventures into my home, limiting my bathroom hours to 7:30 A.M. to 9:00 A.M., Monday through Friday, and 1:00 A.M. to 8:00 A.M. on the weekends. I have considered the idea of erecting a really nice outhouse on the back of my lot, affording me the peace and privacy I feel I've earned after seventeen years of bathroom bonding, but alas, it's rental property and then there's all that red tape to get a zoning variance. Besides, it's only a short drive down the mountain to my low-traffic office bathroom.

Angela D. Conroy is a happily re-married mom in a blended family with six children, four of whom are teenage boys. Needless to say, she is never at a loss for material about raising kids. She writes a monthly column for her community newspaper.

The Broken Foot

Debra Godfrey

There comes a time in your life when you must depend on your children to help you. For me this was always a scary thought. I have four children, ages 3, 7, 9, and 11. And they don't seem to be able to do the littlest thing without me going over it step by step with them. So my biggest fear was what they would do if something happened to me in the house—like if I became unconscious. Would they know what to do? Would they panic and go hysterical? Or, even worse, would they just step over my body all day and then when their father came home say, "I think there is something wrong with Mom. She's been lying around a little more than usual today."

Recently, my question was answered. My children were home from school on one of those teacher in-service days or, as I call them, teacher revenge day. I was walking down the stairs, frantically trying to figure out a way to keep my children busy and maintain my sanity at the same time, and I slipped. When I reached the bottom of the stairs, I could feel the bone break in my foot. I had never broken anything before so this was a brand new experience for me. Oh, goody goody. Two brand new experiences, one living my worst nightmare and the other causing me intense pain. And people wonder why I don't want to try more new things.

I looked around and realized that I was stuck on the landing of my stairs. I could not get up or down the stairs. We did not have a cordless phone. Our neighbors were all at work and my husband was on his way to his office in New York City. I couldn't decide which was worse—having a broken foot or being in my children's hands. I tried to remember how many times I had yelled at them in the last twenty-four hours and who was being punished. I could only pray they would let bygones be bygones and help me.

And so I sat waiting for my children to rescue me...but there was total silence. We were off to a good start. The same children who can hear me in the next room whispering to my husband about their birthday presents completely missed my screams of pain.

"Can someone help me here?" I yelled.

"One second, Mom," my oldest son said, "just let me watch till the next commercial."

"I think I broke my foot," I said.

I could hear my children running toward me from four different directions. They all crowded on the landing, staring at my foot.

"Wow. This is so cool," my nine-year-old son Mike said. "You never do anything exciting."

"Are you going to die?" my seven-year-old son Jeff asked. He is the optimist of the group.

"I'm not going to die," I said. "But I can't get off the stairs, so you are going to have to help me."

"I think you need an ice pack," my eleven-year-old daughter said.

"No, I think it needs to be heated," Mike said.

"How would you know?" my daughter said scornfully. "You got a 'C' in health."

"Mom, which is it?" my son demanded.

"Telephone," I said weakly.

"No, no," my daughter said. "I know it is not a telephone."

"Maybe she is hallucinating," Mike said. "This is so cool."

"People hallucinate just before they die," Jeff said.

"I'm not dying," I screamed. "I need the phone."

"Mommy cranky," my three-year-old son Tommy chimed in.

"Yes, dear, Mommy is cranky because she is in intense pain," I said. "Elizabeth, I want you to call your dad and tell him what happened. Don't panic him. Don't scream in the phone, 'Mom is hurt and she can't move,' or something like that. Just tell him I think I broke my foot and ask him to meet me at the hospital. Then call 911 and tell them to send an ambulance. Do you know our address?"

"Mom, please!"

"All right, then call Aunt Kathy and ask her to come get you guys. Did you get all that?"

"Gotcha, Mom," my daughter said and she ran down the stairs.

"I'll help her," Mike said and ran after her.

"Jeff, could you get me a glass of water?" I asked. He took off.

"I sit wif you, Mommy," Tommy said and promptly sat on my broken foot.

A few minutes later I could hear my son and daughter fighting over who was going to dial the phone.

"She told me to do it," my daughter said.

"I am the calm one. Let me talk to Dad," my son yelled. As the argument escalated I asked them to remember me and my broken foot. I could see myself sitting on the landing all day as my children fought over each phone call.

A little while later, my daughter came back with an ice pack. She put it on my foot. "I called Daddy and he is on his way. He said to tell you that breaking your foot is not a good way of keeping us entertained. Aunt Kathy is also coming. She said this is a sneaky way to get out of teacher revenge day. And the ambulance will be here in a few minutes. Mike, get her a pillow so we can elevate her foot."

A short while later I left for the hospital. I could not believe how calm and efficient my children were. They were actually able to handle a crisis. My daughter was so cool, you would have thought she was dealing with a stranger instead of her mother. She could at least have broken out in a sweat. I would not want to break my foot again, but it was worth it to discover that I could depend on my children when I needed them.

Debra Godfrey writes a humor column for a New Jersey newspaper and lives in Plainsboro, New Jersey, with her husband and four children.

Observations on a Rare Bird

Alice Kolega

It has recently occurred to me that I am a member of an endangered species. Unlike the three-inch snail darter, no conservationists are holding back the flood waters to protect our natural habitat. The genus *Mater Familias Major*, commonly known as mothers of large families, may soon be extinct. Before that time comes, I would like to record some of the peculiar characteristics of this once thriving group, so that if you should encounter one some day, you will know how to handle it. A number of myths have developed over the years which may now be regarded as scientific fact. I would like to differentiate between the myth and the fact.

Myth: Mothers of large families require less sleep than other people.

Fact: Most prolific mothers would give their right arm and one or two of their children for a little more sleep.

I don't think I have slept through a night in twenty-four

years. With the first baby, in addition to night feedings, there is a tendency for the new mother to lie awake listening to the baby breathe. The slightest sigh, gasp, or gurgle will send you hurtling out of bed to find out what dire catastrophe has taken place. Then come the childhood illnesses. Sick children invariably cough and throw up most often between 2:00 and 4:00 A.M., settling down to sleep about the time the newest family member is waking up for another meal. In the years between childhood and sixteen, there is an odd assortment of sleepwalking, bad dreams, falling out of bed, talking in one's sleep, etc. As soon as they are sure you are awake and aware of their problem, they promptly go back to sleep, while you stare at the ceiling waiting for whatever comes next.

Then they get their driver's license and you lie awake waiting for them to get home. Sometimes you fall asleep, they come home and go to bed, and you wake up and spend another hour in panic and rage, until you check and find them sleeping like angels.

To eliminate any possibility of a night with none of the above, there is always a cat who needs to be let out at 3:00 A.M., or a dog who is already out and barking beside a neighbor's window. Just when you think you've come through alive but tired, your married daughter calls at 4:00 in the morning and asks if you would care to join them at the hospital maternity wing.

Myth: Mothers with many offspring like to get up early in the morning.

Fact: They spend the first years of their children's lives sleeping through alarms, missing school busses, being late for work, and sleeping until noon on Saturdays.

Afterward, you get up early only for one or more of the following reasons:

1. It's easier than removing a mixture of minute rice, flour, oatmeal, and maple syrup from the kitchen floor.
2. Your husband is a firm believer in the adage about early to bed, early to rise and classifies sleeping until 7:30 a.m. on weekends as a mortal sin.
3. Your morning paper boy needs a ride because he can't ride his bike through two feet of snow.
4. The phone is ringing. Your ten-year-old's friend wants to know what she is wearing to school.

Myth: Mothers of many are not socially inclined.

Fact: It's easier, cheaper, and less embarrassing to stay home.

At the present rate for baby sitters, it costs big bucks just to get out the door, not counting the cost of whatever activity is planned. The time it takes finding a sitter can set you three weeks behind in your already shaky housework schedule. The reliable ones are invariably booked in advance, whereas you can't plan ahead because you don't know if you will be healthy enough or wealthy enough to go anyplace until the actual day arrives. If they are over sixteen they have "real" jobs and don't want to baby-sit. If they are under sixteen you have to leave early to get home in time for their own curfew. You finally find one who comes highly recommended, but she sleeps so soundly you have to climb through the upstairs window to get inside your house at the end of the night.

Taking the kids along during the daytime is risky at best. For example, your husband's boss's wife invites you for coffee. Your toddler plays very quietly in the bedroom, taking all the boss's socks and underwear out of the dresser and spreading them all over the floor. Or, you go to donate a pint of blood to the Red Cross. Your one-year-old howls until the baby-sitting service returns him and he sits happily on your stomach watching you bleed into a little plastic bag.

Finally you decide to stay home and wait until some of your own grow up so they can baby-sit for you. They start the rumor that they are capable sitters because of their vast experience with younger brothers and sisters and are in such demand that they're never available to you.

As one maternal colleague said, "Let's face it. Where can we go, except to visit each other?"

Myth: Mothers of large families are hoarders by nature.

Fact: The mother is usually the only thrower-outer in a family of packrats.

It's frustrating to be the only one in the family who ever throws anything away. I grew up in a house stuffed with generations of furniture, clothing, and books—especially books. It was a cardinal sin to throw away a book. On the paternal side, everything was saved because you never knew when you might need a paper bag, a Clorox bottle, or a new supply of coat hangers.

Our children have inherited a double set of squirrel genes. I sometimes look at the accumulation of nine people times twenty-five years and feel like the movie heroine who imagined herself standing on the roof in her nightgown screaming at the top of her lungs.

Our collection includes such items as:

All of our old broken appliances, lamps, radios, and record players. Someday someone is going to have the time to tinker with and fix them.

All of my husband's school notes from high school chemistry through Ph.D. dissertation. You never know when you may have to check a source. A kindly worm helped my cause a little by eating through one carton and making the contents illegible.

Five lawn mowers—four of which are inoperable. Their spare parts keep the active one in operation.

A pile of windows from an old barn which was leveled years ago. We might build around them someday.

Every game and stuffed animal which seven children can accumulate from age zero to eighteen, when they no longer use them but can't bear to part with them.

A supply of "priceless" antiques left by the previous owners, who didn't think it worth the bother to take them along.

Thirteen bicycles of varying sizes and speeds, only three of which work and none of which have interchangeable parts.

The only thing I enjoy about moving is the opportunity it affords me to throw things out. Once, I piled things out front on collection day and then watched in amazement as people passing the house stopped to retrieve things from the pile.

Myth: Mothers of mobs enjoy camping vacations.

Fact: What other kind is there? Only Donald Trump could afford to put up nine people in a motel, and visiting friends or relatives would strain even the diplomacy of a UN ambassador.

The head of our household views vacations as a symptom of our decadent society. Vacations for me consisted of eight trips to the hospital—seven to the maternity floor, and one to the surgical department to repair the damage the other seven did to the veins in my legs. Family vacations consisted of traveling over the river and through the woods to you-know-where every Thanksgiving, Christmas, and Easter, and several cross-country jaunts, so that father could go back to school.

The first vacation taken just for the fun of it came after sixteen years and only served to strengthen my husband's conviction that, like idle hands, they are the devil's workshop. On the way, one of the kids got sick, but we thought it was just our usual travel malady which would pass when we reached solid ground. It didn't. It got worse. We hunted up a local doctor who labeled it "the bug," whereupon two more kids took to their sleeping bags.

The healthy ones grew restless, so their father tried to salvage the week for them while I sat in the woods ministering to the sick. Like Moses and the Egyptians, when the plague had run its course, the weather was called in to do battle. While it didn't rain toads and lizards, there was enough water around to make one wonder where all the animals were going two at a time.

Our grown children borrow the tent now frequently, but their father hasn't set foot in it since.

Myth: Mothers of large numbers hate to see their children grow up and leave home.

Fact: They can't wait. The only trouble is that every time one leaves, another comes back.

We need swinging doors at our house. Having a houseful of independent teenagers is interesting, but severely strains the traffic pattern, especially between Memorial Day and Labor Day.

In the spring, the ones who have been away at school begin returning and the ones who have been at home prepare to leave for the summer. The front door has barely stopped swinging when the reverse migration begins in the fall with the addition of one more to the college-bound list. A typical week in August might go something like this:

Middle child calls from California where she spent the summer to say she would like to move back home from her apartment to recoup the money she blew on her vacation.

Ten-year-old sister has two days to move all her toys out of sister's empty room and cram them back into her own room.

High schooler, who moved brother's bed into her room so a friend could spend a week's vacation, has to move it back before he comes home from summer job on Long Island.

Middle child arrives from California, and moves her belongings home from apartment. After two days, she decides that she can't stand it at home, finds another apartment to share, and starts moving out again.

College freshman prepares to leave for freshman orientation in New York City. The day before, he needs three pairs of pants shortened. The scissors are nowhere to be found. In desperation, they have to be cut off with a steak knife.

Two cars break down, leaving one which is urgently needed by at least four people: high school sophomore has to get to part-time job, which is financing a school trip to Germany next year. College freshman must get to bank to withdraw all his savings. Mother must get to store or everyone will starve to death. Father must get to work or they really will starve. Middle child must move out or she will go mad.

Mother considers running away from home.

Now that family sizes range from zero to 1.8 children, you may never have the opportunity to see one of these rare birds. On the chance that you should encounter one, here is a list of dangerous expressions. Mothers of large families have been known to become violent at the following statements:

"I hope I didn't wake you. Were you taking a nap?"

"Why are you cleaning house? Are we having company?"

"There's never anything good to eat in this house."

"You don't work, do you?"

"What did you do all day?"

The recommended approach would be to smile, extend a hot cup of coffee, and exclaim, "I don't know how you do it!"

Alice Kolega is a graduate of Albertus Magnus College and has worked as a social worker, teacher's aide, secretary, and library technician, but mostly as a mother. She is a tutor, grandmother, and reluctant septuagenarian.

Why It Takes Mom a Week to Get Over the 24-Hour Flu

Angela D. Conroy

Ever wonder why it takes Mommy a week to get over the twenty-four-hour flu bug? I'll tell you why. Because:

1. Daddy needs his shirts ironed.
2. Little Tommy is out of clean clothes.
3. There's nothing to eat in the house.
4. You're in charge of the school fund-raiser on Saturday.

This is only day two of the twenty-four-hour flu bug. By day three, your color is gone, your eyes are glazed, your hair is in a constant state of rebellion, and your teeth hurt. And yet you trudge on, getting your rest while you can. (Try draping yourself across your grocery buggy while waiting in the checkout line. This is good for at least twenty minutes at the Red Food Store. Use your bread as your pillow!) By day four, you are starting to lose your motor skills. Your mind is dull and your abdominal pains are sharp! By day five, you realize that not eating anything solid since you can't remember when has left you weak—e.g., your toothbrush feels heavy.

At 2:45 P.M. on day six, the first child hits the front door—

"Hey, Mom! Mom? Mom, where are you?"

"I'm coming, dear."

You stop and recline halfway down the steps to recharge your battery.

"Mom, can I have Buster, Slov, and Killer to spend the night? I promise we won't make any noise!" (This coming from the child who tackles every piece of furniture he passes.)

"Not tonight, honey. I'm not feeling well."

"Well, can they at least stay and play for awhile since they're already here?"

"Fine."

"Come on, guys. Let's go upstairs and play 'Kill the man with the ball.'"

"Hey, was that your Mom we just stepped over lying on the steps?"

"Yeah, she's sick or something. Come on!"

Child No. 2 hits the front door —

"Hey, Mom! Boy, this place is a wreck! Why didn't you clean up today? You still got that flu-thing? Mom, is it alright if the guys come over here to practice band? I told them you wouldn't mind. It'll only take a couple of hours."

By now you are crawling head first down the steps. "If I can only make it outside, I'll lie down in the middle of the street and maybe someone will stop and help me!"

"Gee, Mom, you look pretty bad. And you need to pull down your nightgown, I can see your underpants."

Child No. 3 hits the front door —

"Hey, Mom! I'm home. Mom? Where's Mom? Man, this place is trashed! What's for dinner? When's Dad getting home?" The phone rings.

"Hello."

"Hey, buddy. It's Dad. How's Mom?"

"I don't know, I can't find her."

"Well, tell her that I'm at the golf club and I'll be home in a half hour or so."

Later on that night, God sends an angel of mercy to gently rub your forehead and tuck the covers in around you. You open your eyes ever so slightly and thank her for coming.

"Just answering prayers," she whispers.

"But I forgot to say mine," you reply.

"I know," she smiles, "but your family didn't."

Angela D. Conroy is a happily re-married mom in a blended family with six children, four of whom are teenage boys. Needless to say, she is never at a loss for material about raising kids. She writes a monthly column for her community newspaper.

The Alien at My House

With any child entering
adolescence, one is desperate for
the smallest indication that
the child's problems will never
be important enough for a
television movie.

—*Delia Ephron*

The Alien at My House

Renee Carr

It's the happiest day of your life. You've brought home a miracle, a bundle of joy that you know you'll love forever. This child will look up to you, love you unconditionally, watch every move you make, and model himself after you. And this is exactly how it goes—for about thirteen years.

Then one night, you put him to bed as you have each night of his life. When he wakes up, he appears the same as he did when he went to bed, but he has suddenly become, without warning, a teenager!

You'd think that it would be a gradual change, something that happens over the course of time, and being a gradual change, parents would just ease into a new role with grace and finesse.

But the morning that he wakes up, impossibly, a teenager, you want to back up the truck and send out a search party for the doting child that disappeared suddenly overnight. You want to confront this new alien-like person, demanding in your best high-pitched parent's voice, "Who are you, and what have you done with my child!?"

He, of course, would just look at you with that blank, bored-out-of-his-wits face that is universal among teenagers, and say something like, "Dude, like, I don't know what you're talking about, man."

Then, he would get on the telephone, an appliance that was once used to transport important messages, and sit with it glued to his ear for the rest of his life, sometimes saying nothing at all. When he does speak, he speaks in a code all his own, beginning every sentence with "dude" or "man."

The rest of the conversation may consist of retelling the events of his day to one of his nearest and dearest best friends, repeating the conversation that went on with one of his other nearest and dearest best friends, which sounds something like, "And then she goes, and then I go, and then he goes, and then we both go..."

Then, he retreats to his room, a safe haven, a place where he can be himself, a place where no one is allowed without super-vision, especially parents. It's amazing how a small, once adorably decorated room could suddenly become a hazardous waste site.

Because of peer pressure, teens are forced to make their parents buy certain types of name-brand clothes. They must have a label stating that they paid at least $30 per sweatshirt, $60 per pair of jeans, etc. Upon entering their room, a parent's thinking is that these clothes, costing them a week's wages, should be hung or folded and neatly put away. After all, that's what closets and dressers are for, right? Wrong!

Apparently, the only way that a teenager can find his clothes, the ones that he so desperately needed, is to stack and pile them in the corners of his room. After all, that's what corners are for, right? Now you're getting it! He, and he alone can unscramble and decipher the mountainous mess before you, and he just can't understand what all the fuss is about.

Shame on you for not realizing that there's no room in the six-drawer dresser that you recently bought for him. And the closet? Well, it was plain silly to even consider that as a storage place for, of all things, clothes!

While standing in the middle of a room where even angels fear to tread, you're suddenly shocked out of your reverie by a blast of noise that sets your teeth on edge and your hair on end. It's what your child defines as "music," although to a parent that can be a misleading term.

Music, to us old folks, has a certain rhythm to it. An even balance of bass, and a beat that's, as they used to say on American Bandstand, "easy to dance to."

The stuff blasting from the boombox right now shakes your very core, all sounding the same with a beat of "boom-boom, boom-boom, boom-boom."

Sometimes the rhythm changes, sounding something like, "heeeeey, hoooooo, heeeeey, hoooooo." And the names of the groups now..."Smashing Pumpkins" and "Salt and Pepa." The first time my teen asked for salt n' pepa, that's just what he got. Until I realized that it wasn't condiments he was after.

If you go out to buy a boombox for your teen for Christmas or his birthday, the only requirements that you'll really have to consider are: can the volume be cranked up high enough to reach the other side of town? And can the bass give the house a heartbeat of its own?

Lots of books have been written to aid in raising teens. Some have really great, sound advice. For those that offer useful advice, I wonder if the author, who is usually a psychologist with some pretty significant degrees, would have about, say, four or five years of spare time to put that advice to the test.

Renee Carr lives in DeMotte, Indiana, with husband, two daughters, and too many animals to mention.

Teenonics

Angela D. Conroy

When the boys were little and learning to talk, we would practice pronouncing different objects around the house: light, ball, door, mama, dada. And like most kids, they had quite a few words mastered by kindergarten. All during elementary school their vocabularies increased and their pronunciation improved...until just recently.

I'm not sure exactly what happens to their vocal skills as teenagers. Maybe their tongues grow faster than the rest of their mouths. All I know is I can't understand a word they say anymore. I know they're talking because if I look really hard at them I can see their lips moving—just barely. And I hear muffled sounds coming from their mouths.

All teenagers seem to talk like this and, of course, they can understand each other perfectly. (I don't know how their teachers do it—I can't carry on a simple conversation with them.)

"Charlie, how's school? Is Spanish going okay?"

"Well, I urgh ugh ugh, slur-slur, mumble mumble mumble. Argh, ugh, ugh."

"Excuse me? You lost me after the first two words."

"Mom, he said it's going okay," my younger son says. He's better at this than I am. "He's been using the Spanish Help computer program in the study lab during Z period for extra help. He says he needs to work on his verb tenses more and go over his vocabulary every night, but this next grading period, his average should be a lot better because of all the extra help he's gotten."

"He said all that just then? No way! His lips didn't even move."

I swear I've had more comprehensible conversations with people who were fast asleep.

On occasion, I've had one of these conversations with one of my boys when the only other person present was an adult. Talk about clueless.

"What did he say?"

"I have no idea. His interpreter is hanging out in the driveway with his buddies."

Fortunately, this is yet one more delightful phase of raising teenagers. Now when I hug my boys good-bye as they head out for the evening I say, "Use your manners, pick up after yourselves, and don't forget to enunciate."

I hug on them a little longer and whisper, "Mama's boys are growing up. Remember when you were little and your lips moved when you talked?"

Angela D. Conroy is a happily re-married mom in a blended family with six children, four of whom are teenage boys. Needless to say, she is never at a loss for material about raising kids. She writes a monthly column for her community newspaper.

How to Recognize the
Father of Teenagers

Ina Valeria Doyle

How to recognize the father of teenagers:
- Knows the high school principal's home phone number by heart.
- Doesn't react when the phone rings (it's never for him, unless it's the high school principal).
- Buys everything in bulk.
- Stops automatically and daily at the grocery store to fill cart with milk, bread, and aspirin.
- Pats the undented fenders of his new car lovingly.
- When riding in the car as a passenger, right leg stiffens from continually applying imaginary brake.
- Hides his car keys.

Ina Valeria Doyle is a write, storyteller, and educator from Honeoye Falls, New York.

Queen of the Road

Judith Marks-White

Just when you thought life was going well, you are confronted with the realization that in only three more months your daughter will be old enough to drive.

For years you spent each day picking up and dropping off. Neither rain nor snow nor fevers of 102 degrees kept you from your daily rounds when your kid and everyone else's hurled their bodies into your trusting old auto.

"Hang in there," you told yourself each morning. "Hold on!" you consoled yourself each night. Someday these little tykes will grow up and be able to fend for themselves.

You began to count the days when, once again, you would be able to view life from outside of a car—a day when you could, finally, be a person whose panorama consisted of more than stop signs, mailboxes, and "No Turn on Red."

You even considered getting a part-time job but your life has no part time left in it. The only thing you qualify for is chauffeur, which means doing exactly what you're doing now.

"What did you do today?" your husband asked after coming in from the real world. "I stopped on red. I moved on green. So what else is new?"

Then, without warning, the day came when your child confronted you with the question: "Mom, may I take driving lessons?"

"Driving lessons? Why in the world would you want to do that?"

"So I can borrow the car."

"You mean take our car on the road...by yourself?"

"Didn't you know that one day I would want to get around without you?"

"No, I always thought we'd travel everywhere together."

"You've driven me around long enough, Mom. I want to be like all my friends. I want to get my license."

It is then you realize how fast the years have flown. The day you dreamed about for years is here. You are being "let go" so that someone else—your child—is actually going to get behind the wheel of a car and of all things, drive it herself.

Panic set in. You began to lose sleep. You bit your nails and kept watch at the window until this adolescent who was responsible for all your years as "Queen of the Car Pool" is out on the road with a license that has only a week's worth of fingerprints on it.

Life suddenly took a turn for the worse. Where once you complained about how much you hated driving, at least you were in control. Now you must share your car with someone who claims she can handle the road even though she still hasn't mastered the art of putting the cap on the toothpaste.

"Don't drive over twenty miles an hour," you tell her. "Don't take your eyes off the road. Don't listen to the radio. Don't put on make-up in the rearview mirror." Without a doubt, you have turned into an hysterical facsimile of what was once a relatively normal mother.

"Keep calm," your husband advised when your daughter borrowed the car one night.

"Calm? I am calm. Why do you think I'm not calm?"

"Because your torso has been hanging out the window for forty-five minutes, and it's 30 degrees outside."

"She was supposed to be home at 10, and it's already 10:07."

"She's a little late. It happens."

"She should have phoned."

"She's fine."

"Maybe she had a flat tire."

"She didn't."

"Maybe she's been carjacked."

"Keep guard at the door," he shouted. "I'll call the police."

At 10:15 she walked in, all smiles.

"Hi guys, I know I'm a few minutes late. I apologize."

"Oh," we said in unison. "We didn't even notice."

But you know something is very wrong when, on a snowy, January afternoon your daughter turns to you and asks: "Mom, I need to borrow the car. I want to go over to Mary's house and study."

You bolt from your chair, throw your coat over your shoulder, and halfway out the door, you shout: "You stay home and relax darling. I'll go over to Mary's and study for you!"

Judith Marks-White is a freelance writer whose column, "The Light Touch," appears in The Westport (Connecticut) News.

The YA Return

The finest inheritance you can
give to a child is to allow it to
make its own way, completely on
its own feet.

—*Isadora Duncan*

It's All Greek to Me

Pat Miller

My daughter decided to rush a sorority this fall. I was surprised. She is, after all, the product of a mixed marriage—her father was in the early-'60s, panty-raiding, fraternity generation and I was in the late-'60s, I'll-rush-when-hell-freezes-over generation. Even while dating we argued about the subject. We once fixed up his roommate and "Greek brother" with my sister and all four of us argued.

My daughter decided to rush a sorority in spite of the fact that she went to her first get-out-the-vote rally when she was two months old and her first Equal Rights Amendment rally at the age of two. And in true '60s fashion I have always shared comments like: "Why join an organization that excludes people based on the most superficial first impressions of appearance, economic class, and social standing?" (My children were never surprised by this kind of language because in their formative years I also threw food at the television set during all eight of Ronald Reagan's State of the Union addresses.)

It should also be pointed out that her father's progressive politics survived his Greek years, so he would counter my arguments about elitism with, "Now, a lot of things have changed. There are opportunities for leadership development, meeting new friends, and…" I always finished for him, "…going to great parties?" Not that I have anything against great parties. I just don't think you should form organizations for the purpose of throwing great parties and then leave some people out.

And while the leadership opportunities sound good, couldn't the same be said for becoming a Tupperware sales rep? There would be just as many parties, and a lot more storage containers to show for your efforts.

Anyway, before and after Rush Week, I was struck by the number of my non-Greek family and friends who had Greek offspring, so I started collecting examples of our prejudices and our ignorance of the process—especially the failure to learn Greek letters.

A neighbor, when asked which sorority her daughter had been in, could only answer, "A big brick one on the corner." ("Still in denial?" I suggested.)

A co-worker, when asked the same thing, said, "One of those with an A in it." (My husband hissed, "They all have A's in them!")

My cousin answered that question with: "I think she's a Sigma Chi, or maybe that's my ex-husband's fraternity." ("It's a fraternity," my husband hissed again, "Remember the song?")

One friend asked me about my daughter, "Does she have big hair and nails yet?" ("No," I said. But perhaps I should measure her head during visits home just to be sure there are no changes.) One reporter friend wondered, "Does this mean she's required to mate with a fraternity person?" (I checked the parents' handbook and there are no specifics about mating rituals.)

Was there some social significance to this trend? Were all our children going to become Rush Limbaugh fans or have there been real changes in the Greek system? Was joining a house just another way to show independence from parents, like dreadlocks and pierced body parts? Anyway, you can see that I came to this subject with a negative attitude and little support. But then a few people stepped forward with suggestions designed to open my mind. One friend whose daughter had pledged the previous year was particularly sympathetic.

This woman was so anti-Greek in her college days that she and several classmates mockingly formed the Gomer Gomer Gomer sorority, printed t-shirts with a triangle and three G's for an insignia, and scrubbed up a rock as an official mascot. Even this former Gomer opted for the good-opportunities-for-leadership-training, learning-organizing-skills, and dealing-with-a-variety-of-social-situations defense and encouraged her daughter to join. Of course she'll be excommunicated from the Gomers for that one.

Even a friend who was the rejected double legacy of her mother's and sister's sorority in 1962—and as a legacy you are supposed to be taken unless you have committed some unspeakable crime like having sex with sheep or wearing white shoes after Labor Day—endorses the "leadership opportunity" defense and mentions positive examples she has seen from her position in university administration. (By the way, she never mentioned whether it was the sheep or the shoes that did her in with the sorority.)

Then, an activist friend revealed that she too had been a Greek and proud of it. I have worked for years on campaigns and causes with this woman, never suspecting she was a card-carrying member of the good-opportunities-for-leadership crowd. She also named other progressive women on the national scene who were Greek, and none of them had big hair and nails! So what's a person with definite—some would say extreme—opinions to do but give a little on this one?

I am feeling better after a discussion with my daughter. She has assured me that she will work for the passage of the Equal Rights Amendment when the opportunity arises and not limit her dates to young men with good haircuts who wear baseball caps. In fact, she says some of her best friends are art majors with beards and ripped jeans.

Actually, I am proud that my daughter chose to do something I would never have dreamed of doing—for her own good reasons. And maybe some things really are changing. My cousin tells me that her daughter's entire sorority got their ankles tatooed recently. Leadership development and body art—what more could a mother ask for?

Pat Miller runs the lectures program for a major midwestern university.

It's Hard to Say Goodbye

Effin Older

I think about it a lot lately, trying to imagine what it will be like. The worst time is in the middle of the night when I wake up from a deep sleep and it's the first thing on my mind. I feel silly crying, but that's what I usually do. Just for a few minutes. Then I go back to sleep.

My husband is much better about these things than I am. He never worries about anything. He says I worry enough for both of us. It's not that I worry, exactly—it's just that I think about things in advance. This time I'm thinking ahead about four months, because that's when it's going to happen.

And because I'm the sort of person who thinks about things in advance, I know that four months can pass very quickly. Then, there you are, face to face for the first time with the thing you should have been dealing with for the past four months.

One of the results of my advance thinking is that I am no longer bothered by things that used to annoy me. For example, finding one of my best bath towels forever spotted with black henna, or having to clean the bathroom hand basin of gritty apricot scrub before I brush my teeth, I simply smile and treasure the memory.

I find myself buying little surprises when I go shopping, knowing that in just four months there won't be anyone to buy silly little things for. I lend my clothes and listen to loud music I don't even like, just because soon no one will be asking to borrow my clothes or playing music for the whole neighborhood to hear.

I mentioned to my accountant, also a mother, what I'd been thinking about recently. She laughed. "Oh, I made it through the first week with no problem."

"Did it take just a week?" I asked with relief. Even I could stand it for a week.

She laughed again. "Oh no! That was just the beginning. I collapsed at the end of the first week."

I felt sick. "Then what did you do?"

"Well, I started working full time, my husband and I ate out a lot, and gradually I pulled myself back together." She squeezed my shoulder. "It isn't easy, but you can do it."

I thanked her for her confidence and asked if she knew of any job vacancies coming up in four months.

Meanwhile, I'm taking other precautionary steps. We became

"parents" of a two-month-old Husky. I don't need any deep psychological interpretation to know that this white, cuddly ball of fluff is related to future events.

I wrote to a dear friend and mentioned the conversation with my accountant. "Don't worry about the empty nest," she wrote back. "You have very important things that your children know and love and need—things that they will keep coming back for—the car, food, money, the car, food...they come back when they're sick of the mess and everyone in their flat. They bring you their every crisis. It's daily contact, you'll be weaned off it gradually."

Recently, my mother told me that she resolved not to cry when my youngest brother, her sixth child, graduated from high school. And she would have made it through the whole ceremony, too, if someone hadn't said, "Well, Mrs. Lawes, how are you feeling? Your baby's leaving home."

"That did it," my mother said. "I felt so foolish, but I couldn't stop crying." She laughed as she recalled the embarrassment she still felt twelve years later. "Of course, I was proud that he was graduating and going on to college, and of course I wanted him to go out into the world and make something of himself. But, on the other hand, he was the last one to go. He was the baby. Even losing the other five didn't make it any easier."

"So what did you do, Ma?"

"I got used to it after a while. I had to, and you will too." I know everything my mother said is true. I know I'd be terribly unhappy if they weren't graduating and going on to college. I know I'd think something was wrong if they weren't excited about leaving home. I know it's time for them to find their own niches in the world.

I know all that. But even so, when my twin daughters, my only children, pack their trunks for college, I'll remember my friends' words. "Don't worry about the empty nest." But I'll feel my mother's words, "I couldn't stop crying." And I'll be crying too.

Effin Older became a writer and photographer after seeing her twin daughters off to college.

The Dreadlock Suite: Tales to Relieve a Mother's Distress

Shirlee Sky Hoffman

1. Introduction: Creation ex neglectio.

We have a major, jumbo hotdog-sized dreadlock living in our house. Residing at the back of our sapling son's head, it is, thank goodness for small mercies, functionally obscured by his gorgeous, curly ponytail.

This dreadlock, like all dreadlocks, is a mass of matted, tangled hair. Unlike some, say the ones on the heads of reggae players, this dreadlock was formed naturally, without the use of artificial aids such as assorted animal dungs.

"I've got a really nice dreadlock forming," our son had announced one evening during a phone call from his summer job in the north woods of Wisconsin.

Not knowing what a dreadlock was, I ignored the announcement.

"My dreadlocks are really doing nicely," our son commented during a later call. "I have two of them."

This time I inquired more closely. His response was neither obvious nor comforting to the uninitiated. "They're called dreadlocks because mothers dread them."

When our son stepped off the bus at the end of the camping season, I finally became clear on the concept. Through histrionics too ugly to detail, I managed to have the number of dreadlocks extant in our family reduced to one. The other, beneficiary of my longstanding but previously only weakly tested commitment to personal freedom in matters of appearance, grows on.

But I don't have to like it.

2. Unintended consequences protect the grandchildren.

Wassim-the-harem-administrator's entire staff went on strike. He answered their job action with a series of well-placed counter-strikes, employing his consummately sharpened scimitar. While effectively getting his point across, Wassim's management style had a predictable short-term downside. He alone was left to tend the sultan's demanding bevy of beauties.

Desperate, Wassim ran out into the street. His eyes darted left, right, up, down, left, right, left again. There. Just what he needed. A naive young American trekker who had no inkling of the basic requirements for working in a seraglio. Wassim prayed the scum was hungry enough.

"Hey, kid. You want to earn some easy dough?"

"Maybe. Doing what?"

"My kitchen staff all came down with the flu. Real sudden. Forty gorgeous, curvaceous girls are coming to my restaurant for a bridal shower. I need help making and serving dinner. Not so hard, and I pay well. Enough for you to live on for a week."

"I've got a gig at a jazz club tonight. Will I be finished by midnight?"

"Yes, it will all be finished by midnight."

"Sure."

Wassim took the American's arm and gently nudged him in the direction of the palace. "Just a few steps, around the corner," he murmured reassuringly.

When the youth turned, something caught Wassim's eye. "Aiee," he squealed, throwing his arms up in the air. "What is that at the back of your head? I have never seen anybody with a second one there."

"Hey man, that's my dreadlock. Three years old this summer. Nice huh?"

"Aiee!! A deadlock. A deadlock. I will have to remove it too! The master would never allow that in among his women. It would lock my death, that deadlock. Aiee!!"

"No job is worth losing my dreadlock," said the American. "And what do you mean, you'll have to remove it too?"

Suddenly very uneasy, he swung around. "Go find someone else to serve your bridal shower," he spat as he sped off into the crowd.

"Aiee," wailed Wassim. "I am lost. I should have kept my mouth shut. But something that disgusting I have never seen before."

3. Nursing nostalgia.

There was a little boy
Who had a second toy
Hanging from the back of his top head.

When he was good
He kept it in its hood
And when he was bad
He was florid.

4. A fashion sensation.

Bienvenue, welcome, mesdames et messieurs, ladies and gentlemen, to our exciting fashion show, showcasing new hair styles for the now generation.

Our first presentation down the walkway this afternoon comes to us from North America, melting pot of the world, where the raw spirituality of deepest, drought-ridden Africa has mixed with the raw masculinity of the wetlands of northern Wisconsin to produce the exquisite hairstyle on our first model.

Peekaboo versatility is the surprise hallmark of this young man's coiffeur, painstakingly nurtured for years before it reached the full, glorious zenith you see before you today.

As he walks slowly down into your midst, please notice the delightfully curly low-slung ponytail, harmoniously set off by the hair pulled tight against the rest of the skull. The casually crooked part, meandering down the middle of the crown, deliciously enhances the overall impression of moderate but still unquestionably presentable unconventionality.

Stop for a moment, young sir, and show our audience the bodacious surprise you are concealing from them.

Voilà ladies and gentlemen, mesdames and messieurs. What do you see when this handsome specimen lifts his ponytail? A fully developed, eternally and gordianly knotted dreadlock.

No ordinary dreadlock, this unsuspected bonus boasts a subtle L-shaped bend one-third of the way up from the bottom. Very difficult to achieve, I assure you. Uniformly round all the way from tip to root, this is a magnificent dreadlock, one that any mother's son would be proud to call his own.

Let's hear a round of thunderous applause for this cunningly complex, cutting-edge hair design. What a viewing privilege has been ours today!

5. To marry or knot.

Once upon a time, in a far off land, there lived a king and a queen who had a handsome, brave, brilliantly clever young son. "The time has come, our son," said the king and the queen, speaking perfectly in unison as always, "to find you a bride."

"Yes, my parents," answered the prince. "But she must be a very special person. She must pass a diabolically difficult test. She must untangle my dreadlock without hurting me."

"That is a perfect test," said the king and queen. "Only a woman who can untangle your dreadlock painlessly is worthy to be your bride. We will declare an open season on your dreadlock for the next four months. That should be enough time. Get it all settled before the first snows fall."

When the young women of the realm heard the proclamation announcing the bridal contest, they lined up before the gates of the castle. Each one carried a sack slung over her shoulder and a smile of hope on her face. Each believed her innovative technique was sure to win the prince.

One by one, the women were admitted to the inner court-yard of the castle. Most solicitously, one by one, they were shown up to the prince's room. There, for three full hours every morning, the prince sat patiently, on a high-backed chair in the middle of the room, blindfolded by a velvet sleep mask. His dreadlock, fetchingly framed by his raven black hair, hung down, unencumbered, against the rich antique cream satin brocade upholstery.

One by one, the women approached the chair. Each one opened her sack to retrieve her special combs and carefully formulated, environmentally friendly detangling lotions and sprays. Each one took a deep breath as she prepared herself to begin the test.

One by one, the women's faces dropped: at the merest glancing touch of his dreadlock, the prince let out an impatient yelp of pain.

After three months, the king and queen began to despair of ever having a daughter-in-law. No more women lined up at the gates of the palace. All the eligible women in the realm, all the eligible women in the neighboring realms, and all the eligible women in the realms neighboring the neighboring realms had tried to untangle the prince's dreadlock without hurting him, and failed.

Even the prince was feeling discouraged. Perhaps he had been too clever in devising the bridal test. Still, he had spent years growing his dreadlock to its present magnificent state. How could he ally himself for life with someone who could not demonstrate, through her gentleness and ingenuity, her appreciation of its symbolic significance for his core identity?

One week, two weeks, three weeks longer, the prince sat in his chair every morning, blindfolded, waiting in vain for another young woman to attempt the bridal test.

By the fourth day of the fourth week of the fourth month, the prince had almost completely resigned himself to being a bachelor. He no longer listened eagerly for footsteps at the door. His full attention was turned inward, contemplating his dreary future: always a best man, never a groom.

Snip! What was that?

The prince jerked his head forward. It felt horribly lighter. Frantically he patted the back of his head. His dreadlock! It was gone! In between the two wings of curly hair flowing down his back was a gaping space.

"What the…!" yelled the prince. Ripping off the sleep mask, he jumped up out of his chair and whirled around to face his attacker. "Who are you and how dare you cut off my dreadlock?" he roared, menacing her with his fist.

"Just cool it," she said, counter-menacing with her scissors. "I'm a contestant in your bridal contest, from four realms over. My horse gave out about a month ago. I was afraid I wasn't going to get here before the deadline. But I did and I still have three whole days to untangle this piece of crap. Relax. You won't feel a thing." And then she smiled the most beautiful smile.

The prince hesitated, just a moment, and then he smiled his prize-winning smile back.

When the king and queen came scurrying into the room to investigate the commotion, they were astonished to see their son and a foreign woman sitting cross-legged on the floor. Their heads bent together, the two of them were painstakingly untangling the dreadlock.

"I'm responsible for getting my hair into this mess," said the prince. "It's only fair that I help straighten it out. Mom and Dad, meet my future wife."

Of course, they all lived happily ever after.

Shirlee Sky Hoffman lives in Chicago and is now fixated on the holes in her daughter's jeans.

The Scent of Cash

Mary A. Harding

My husband and I have been blessed with three wonderful children. They are all healthy, happy individuals, each with strengths of his or her own. Our oldest son is a math whiz, our daughter is an artist, and our youngest son has a very unique talent. He is able to smell money.

Andy's particular talent came to light early in his life, and it has continued down through the years. His sensitivity to cash has alerted him to the presence of tax refunds, raises, and the five dollars I might have remaining in the checking account at the end of the week. He lifts his nose, sniffs the air, and knows there is cash around. He also has the uncanny ability to have a pressing expense exactly equal to the amount of the surplus.

When it came time for Andy to leave for college, I began to nurture a false sense of security. Eighty-five miles was a good distance. Not so. He was able to sniff out the twenty dollars I saved on grocery shopping the first week he went away. Even when he transferred to another college fifteen hundred miles away, it made no difference, except now his cash emergencies were often larger than the supposed "surplus." Amazingly, the tantalizing odor of greenbacks can transcend any distance.

I have great hopes for Andy's future job opportunities. His destiny lies in the skill of his nose. It is not unlike the dexterity of truffle-sniffing pigs. Perhaps he could seek employment with oil or mining companies. Imagine the funds they could save if they didn't have to dig randomly; by hiring my son and his nose, they would know the exact spot in which to locate an important find. Archaeologists and anthropologists would seek him out. He could be an invaluable resource to the government. The possibilities are endless.

With all this opulence looming in the future, I ask myself will he still be after my cash? Perhaps I will be relegated to the role of small potatoes. Andy seems to have found the real route to success in life. All it takes is a good set of nostrils.

Mary A. Harding is a middle school teacher, writer, and the mother of three children. As the holder of the family purse strings, she has discovered that the demand for monetary disbursements never lessens, no matter the age of the child.

The YA Return

Ina Valeria Doyle

I am not talking about a special book drop for Young Adult novels. These are the real thing—the young adults themselves.

Households across the nation are seeing the return of the YAs. As changes in the economy dictate, they are returning from college dormitories to household bedrooms, from far off campuses to local job facilities, from job training to job seeking, from a stint in the services to testing skills in the civilian world; but wherever they are coming from, they're all coming home!

Parents who lived through the teen years were learning new behavior patterns before the YA return began. It was a time to rediscover steak for two instead of hamburger for six. It was a time to hear the telephone ringing and believe that it might be for one of them. It was a time to relax at home as a couple, not a group.

It is a shame that we have no term for the grown-up off-spring—other than grown-up offspring. I can write it, but I can't use it in the average supermarket conversation.

I am talking about the in-between young person who has not quite gone, but close enough. This person is still semi-dependent, but has had a taste of adult life. The parents have had a taste of non-parenting. Some new coping mechanisms should be tried rather than dragging out the old ones used on younger teenagers.

If the tight economy has forced them home, it may force them to share the family car with you. This sharing may lead to sleep disturbances until a curfew is firmly established. A curfew for the YA is optional, but for the car it is a necessity. A clear understanding that the offspring are truly loved more than the car is tricky. Try the following approach:

"Honey, we trust you. Could you call home regularly to let us know how the car is?" Thus, the most frequently asked question after, "May I borrow the car?" becomes, "What time does the car have to be home?" (I did not say it was a great idea, but it works!)

Telephones are of major importance in YA homes. You will need to keep an accurate record of all phone messages. (Remember, the next phone call you take could be a job offer for one of those YAs. Keep that hope alive—it will take you through a twenty-phone-call evening.)

Your typical phone message sheet may be the following type:

Pete,
Mary called at 7:15. Call her back. URGENT!
Love ya,
Mom
She called again at 8:00. At 8:30 and 9:05.
PLEASE TALK TO HER AGAIN ABOUT
ALL THESE CALLS.

(Mary's messages are always URGENT to Mary, but not to Pete.)

A Sign-In sheet becomes a true part of the family routine when it looks like this:

Pete home at 10:30.
Please wake me EARLY for work.
Fred, Sheila, and Nan home at 12:00.
Where are Mom and Dad?
Mom and Dad in at 1:30.
Love ya,
Mom

Sign-In sheets are reminiscent of college days of the '50s and earlier. Maybe the financially pressed universities with empty dorm space are missing a real opportunity. YAs across the nation might be willing to pool their meager monies to provide parents with a semester of dorm life. It would give the parents a chance to "find themselves" away from home. It might remind them, too, what it is like to come home to a changed household.

Sending parents away might be a bit drastic. Yet, if the job market doesn't loosen up and longer school recesses continue, start looking for more of the following ads:

LOST

TWO PARENTS

Last seen wearing T-shirts with the logo
"Whatever Happened to the Empty Nest?"
Believed to be runaways.
Contact this paper.
MEAGER REWARD OFFERED

You may laugh, but the tactic used more often than parental running away is parental selling of the family home. (It is thoughtful to leave some sort of forwarding address.)

Ina Valeria Doyle is a write, storyteller, and educator from Honeoye Falls, New York.

Mother Voices uses the heartfelt words of nearly one hundred women to reveal the varied stages of motherhood in all its glory and stresses. Through very personal stories, this book captures the identity and lifestyle changes that come with the challenges of being "Mommy."

ISBN 1-887166-45-9; $12.95 U.S.

Sourcebooks books are available and bookstores everywhere, or by calling 630-961-3900.

Take Good Care of Me

What Kids Think Every Grown-up Needs to Know About Being a Parent

Created By
Kari Cimbalik

With candor and insight, in artwork and original writing, children have a compelling message for grown-ups.

- What should parents know about kids?
- What is the most important thing parents should teach their children?
- How can a mother or father be better parents?

ISBN: 1-57071-442-8; $9.95 U.S.

Sourcebooks books are available and bookstores everywhere, or by calling 630-961-3900.

Dear Mommy and Dear Daddy coupon books are gifts children can give to thank parents for their hard work, patience, and love. There are coupons for helping to clean up after meals, sitting up straight, sharing nicely, and spending special moments together.

ISBN: 1-57071-448-7; $5.95 U.S. (Dear Mommy)

ISBN: 1-57071-451-7; $5.95 U.S. (Dear Daddy)

Sourcebooks books are available and bookstores everywhere, or by calling 630-961-3900.